ENGLISH-LANGUAGE LEARNERS

STUDENT HANDBOOK

Harcourt
SCHOOL PUBLISHERS

www.harcourtschool.com

Requests for permission to make copies of any part of the work should be addressed to School Permissions and Copyrights, Harcourt, Inc., 6277 Sea Harbor Drive, Orlando, Florida 32887-6777. Fax: 407-345-2418.

STORYTOWN is a trademark of Harcourt, Inc. HARCOURT and the Harcourt Logo are trademarks of Harcourt, Inc., registered in the United States of America and/or other jurisdictions.

Printed in the United States of America

ISBN 10 0-15-367055-X

ISBN 13 978-0-15-367055-8

1 2 3 4 5 6 7 8 9 10 197 16 15 14 13 12 11 10 09 08 07

CONTENTS

CONTENTS

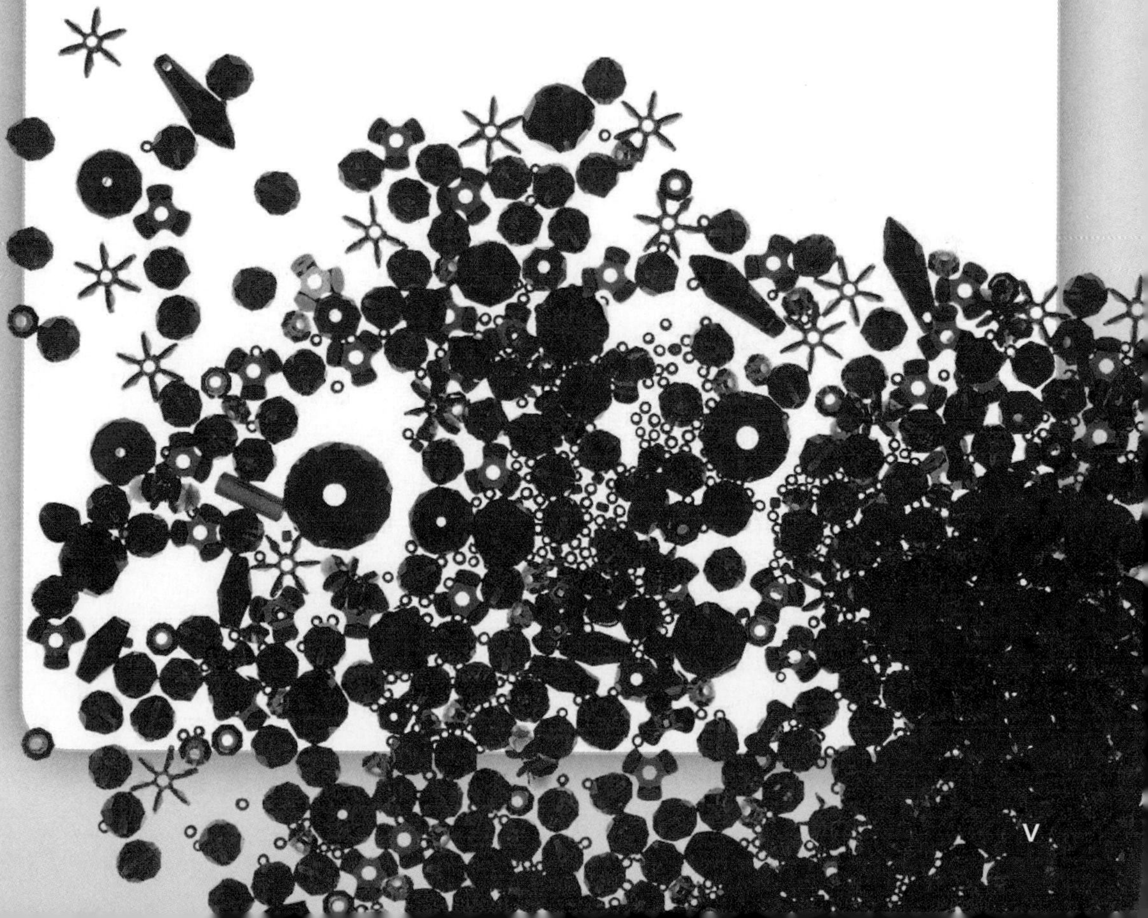

Use What You Know

You can use what you know to help you understand what you read.

Wolves are part of the dog family, but they live in the wild. Wolves are very smart animals. They live in packs and hunt together. Wolves can smell things and hear things from far away.

- **Think about expressions**
  "I think *live in packs* means that wolves live together."

- **Use prior knowledge**
  "I know what dogs look like. Wolves must look like dogs."

- **Reason**
  "If wolves can hear things and smell things from far away, they are probably good hunters."

Find Help

If you need help understanding what you read, look around you.

Whales are mammals that live in the ocean. They look like giant fish. There are many kinds of whales. Some whales can weigh as much as twenty elephants.

- **Use a computer**
  "A computer can help me learn more about whales."

- **Use books**
  "The encyclopedia says that mammals are warm-blooded animals."

- **Ask for help**
  "I can ask a teacher, friend, or family member how to say the word *mammals*."

Make Connections

Try to make connections between what you read and your own experience.

Katie can't wait to visit her grandparents in Maine. She lives in Florida, where it is warm most of the year. It is autumn now, so Katie's grandparents remind her to bring a sweater.

- **Reuse language**
"I say *I can't wait* when I'm excited about something. I think Katie is excited to visit her grandparents."

- **Use synonyms**
Another word for *lives* is *resides*. Another way to say *autumn* is *fall*.

- **Compare and contrast**
Maine and Florida both have beaches. Maine is colder than Florida, and people need heavier clothing in fall.

Picture It

Making pictures in your mind can help you understand.

When my brother was a baby, he did not have hair. He couldn't speak, either. I was much bigger than he was. Now my brother has thick brown hair. He never stops talking, and he is very tall!

- **Make pictures in your mind**
  as a baby . . .
  now . . .

- **Describe it**
  "Telling someone else about a subject can help me picture it and remember it."

- **Use actions**
  "I can raise my arm to show how tall someone is."

Look for Patterns

Looking for words and word parts that are the same can help you understand what you read.

> This old man, he played one,
> He played knick-knack on my thumb,
> With a knick-knack, paddy whack,
> Give the dog a bone,
> This old man came rolling home.
>
> This old man, he played two,
> He played knick-knack on my shoe,
> With a knick-knack, paddy whack,
> Give the dog a bone,

- **Use rhyme**
  "*Knack* and *whack* both have *ack*. I am sure they rhyme. Knowing *knack* will help me read *whack*."

- **Use repetition**
  "*Give the dog a bone* repeats in this rhyme. I think *This old man came rolling home* also repeats."

- **Think about word families**
  "I know the letters *kn* in the word *knee* stand for the *n* sound. I can use this to read the words *knick* and *knack*."

Set a Purpose

Think about what you want to learn or tell.

Exercise is good for you. Team sports can make exercising fun for everyone. Some people enjoy playing basketball, football, or soccer. No matter what sport you like best, all sports are a good way to exercise.

- **Purpose for reading**
  "I want to find out about ways to exercise."

- **Purpose for speaking**
  "I want to get people to sign up for a team sport."

- **Purpose for writing**
  "I want to write a report about team sports."

- **Purpose for listening**
  "I will listen to find out more about exercise."

Background and Vocabulary

Selections You Will Read

• "Ruby the Copycat"
• "The Singing Marvel"

"Ruby the Copycat" is realistic fiction.
Realistic Fiction
• has a beginning, a middle, and an end
• has characters and a setting that could be real

What is "Ruby the Copycat" about?

This story is about a girl named Ruby who tries to be just like another girl in her new class.

A copycat is a person who tries to look or act like someone else.

Hopping is a kind of jumping or bouncing. You can hop on one foot or with both feet.

hopping ▶

◀ copycat

2

What vocabulary will you learn?

Robust Vocabulary

coincidence

pleasant

modeled

murmured

loyal

recited

Tip

Be a Word Detective! Look for these words in newspapers, magazines, and books. Listen for the words on the radio of television.

sneakers

Word Bank

bow

picnic table

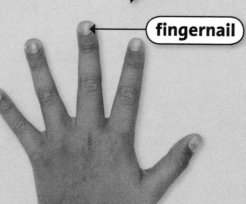

fingernail

sweater

3

Phonics and Spelling

Look at these words:

sat	bed	did	top	pup

Read the words aloud. Listen to the vowel sounds.
The **short vowels** are *a, e, i, o,* and *u.* Some words
with **short vowel** sounds have a CVC pattern.

◄ The **cat** is **black.**

The **cups** are **red.** ▶

Grammar and Writing
What is the grammar skill?

You will learn about **sentences.** Some sentences **tell.**
Some sentences **ask.**

Telling Sentence ⟷ **Ruby likes to hop.**

Asking Sentence ⟷ **When does Ruby hop?**

Comprehension

What is the focus skill in this lesson?

The focus skill is **Narrative Elements**.
Characters and **Setting** are two narrative elements.

To understand narrative elements:

• Ask, "Who are the characters (the people or animals in the story)?"

• Ask, "What is the setting (the time and place that the story happens)?"

Read the passage.

> After school, Amy, Max, and Sara went to the Learning Center. They studied for their math test. "I'm having fun!" said Max.

The characters are Amy, Max and Sara. The setting is after school at the Learning Center.

Background and Vocabulary

Selections You Will Read

- "The Day Eddie Met the Author"
- "Good Books, Good Times"

"The Day Eddie Met the Author" is **realistic fiction**. Realistic Fiction

- has a setting that is real or could be real
- has characters who behave like real people

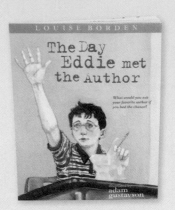

What is "The Day Eddie Met the Author" about?

This story is about a boy named Eddie who meets a real author at his school.

An **author** is someone who writes. Authors write books, reports, or other texts.

author ▶

What vocabulary will you learn?

Robust Vocabulary

assembly

plenty

dismiss

squirmed

patchwork

autographed

Tip

Remember to look in the Glossary for explanations of the words. What other strategies can you use?

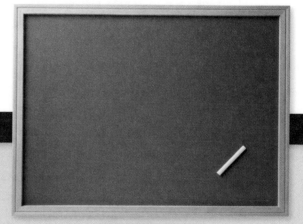

Word Bank

pencil

chalkboard

notebook

vest

Phonics and Spelling

Look at these words:

The **root word** *wait* is in all three sentences. The endings *-ed* and *-ing* have been added to the end of the word. These word endings tell when something happens.

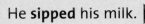

| wait | waited | waiting |

Read the words aloud.
Sometimes the spelling of the word changes when you add *-ed* and *-ing*.

He **sipped** his milk. ▶

The girl is **running.** ▶

Grammar and Writing

What is the grammar skill?

You will learn more about **sentences**. Some sentences are **commands**. Sentences that are **exclamations** show strong feelings.

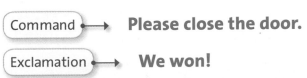

Command ⟶ **Please close the door.**

Exclamation ⟶ **We won!**

Comprehension

What is the focus skill in this lesson?

The focus skill is **Narrative Elements. Characters** and **Setting** are two narrative elements.

To understand narrative elements:

- Ask, "Who are the characters (the people or animals in the story)?"
- Ask, "What is the setting (the time and place that the story happens)?"

Read the passage.

> Danny had been waiting for this day all year. The snow was deep and the hill outside his house was waiting for him. He grabbed is red snow disk and ran outside.

The character in the story is Danny. The setting is the snowy hill outside his house.

Background and Vocabulary

Selections You Will Read
- "Schools Around the World"
- "Keys to the Universe"

"Schools Around the World" is **expository nonfiction**. Expository Nonfiction
- has text divided into sections
- has headings that tell about each section

What is "Schools Around the World" about?

This selection tells how schools around the world are different and how they are the same.

When we say **all around the world**, we mean the cities, towns, and villages in different countries.

world ▼

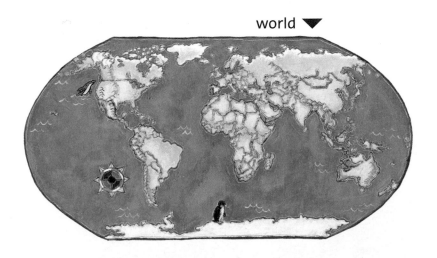

What vocabulary will you learn?

Robust Vocabulary

chores

certain

resources

culture

tutor

uniforms

Word Bank

Tip
Be a World Detective! Look for these words in newspapers, magazines, and books. Listen for the words on the radio or television.

bicycle

train

car

bus

computer

11

Phonics and Spelling

Some **long vowel** sounds are made when two vowels are together.

| train | play | read | grow |

Read the words aloud. Listen for the **long vowel** sounds. Look at how these sounds are spelled.

tree ▶

Long Vowel Sound	Spelling
/ā/	ai as in rain ay as in stay
/ē/	ee as in green ea as in bead
/ō/	oa as in oats ow as in show

▼ boat   pail ▶

Grammar and Writing
What is the grammar skill?

You will learn about **subjects** and **predicates**.
A subject tells who or what the sentence is about.
A **predicate** shows what the subject is or does.

(subject) (predicate)

The happy children go to school.

Comprehension

What is the focus skill in this lesson?

The focus skill is **Locate Information: Book Parts, Text Features.** Captions and headings can help you **locate information** in nonfiction.

To understand how to locate information, remember:

- A **caption** tells about photographs, illustrations, maps, and charts.
- A **heading** is the title of a certain part of a book. It tells what you will find in that part of the book.

Read the passage.

The Blue Morpho buterfly can be found in the rainforests of Central and South America. It has bright blue wings. The wings have a brown border. The body is also brown.

The caption tells about the photograph.

This is a Blue Morpho butterfly.

Background and Vocabulary

Selections You Will Read
• "Ellen Ochoa, Astronaut"
• "What's in the News?"

"Ellen Ochoa, Astronaut" is a biography.
Biography:
• has facts about a person's life
• has dates and place-names

What is "Ellen Ochoa, Astronaut" about?

This selection is about the life of Ellen Ochoa, the first Hispanic woman in space.

Space is the place outside of the planet Earth. The stars and moon are in space.

An astronaut is somebody trained to travel and work in space.

space ▶

astronaut ▶

What vocabulary will you learn?

talented

apply

research

invention

hinder

disappointed

Tip

As you learn new words, remember to write them in your Vocabulary Log. Which words do you know very well? Which words are you still learning?

Word Bank

flute

plane

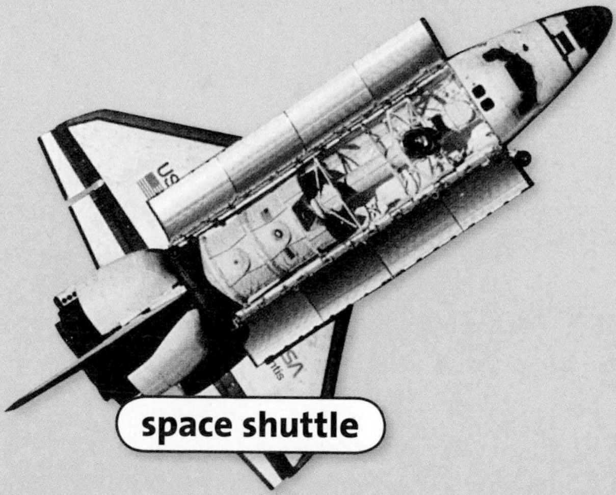

N26732

space suit

moon

space shuttle

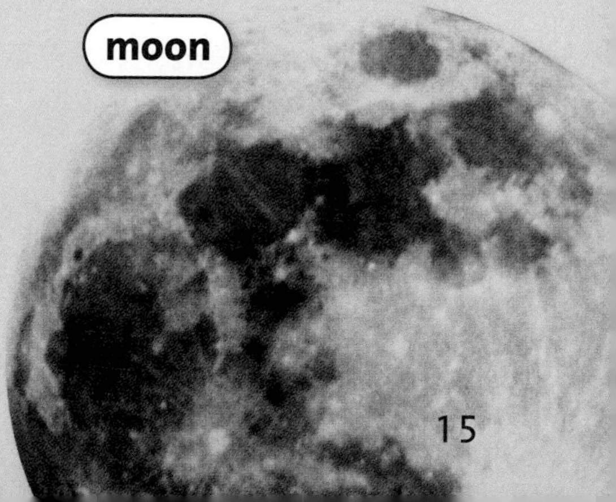

Phonics and Spelling

Look at these words:

The letter *s* is added to show more than one. This is called a **plural.** Words ending with the letters *ss, x, ch,* and *sh* are made **plural** by adding *-es.* If a word ends with a consonant and *y*, change the *y* to *i* and add *-es.*

pencil	pencils

Read the words aloud. Look at how the plurals are made.

peaches ▶

◀ pennies

Grammar and Writing

What is the grammar skill?

You will learn about **compound subjects** and **predicates. Compound** means two or more. **Compound subjects** are two or more subjects in a sentence. **Compound predicates** are two or more predicates in a sentence.

Boys and girls jump and run.

compound subject   compound predicate

16

Comprehension

What is the focus skill in this lesson?

The focus skill is **Locate Information: Book Parts, Text Features.** Some book parts help you find information.

To understand how to locate information, remember:

- A **table of contents** shows how a book is organized. It is at the beginning of the book.
- An **index** lists people, places, and topics in a book with page numbers. It is at the end of the book.

Read the passage.

Franklin is learning about space. He wants to read about astronauts. He looks in the index to find pages in the book that are about astronauts.

Franklin looks in the index of his book.

Background and Vocabulary

Selections You Will Read

You will read a selection titled "The School News." The selection is a **Readers' Theater.**

You will also read a selection titled "I Live in a Town." This selection is **nonfiction**. Nonfiction gives facts or other true information. It is organized using features such as headings, photographs, and captions.

What are the selections about?

"The School News" gives a news report about the school lunch, the weather, a soccer game, and other events.

"I Live in a Town" tells about one child's town and some of the things that make it special.

▼ the news

a reporter ▶

What vocabulary will you learn?

Robust Vocabulary

viewers

survive

camouflage

concealed

independent

donated

Tip

Be a Word Detective! Look for these words in newspapers, magazines, and books. Listen for the words on the radio or television.

Word Bank

puddle

frog

poodle

soccer

 # Fluency

As you read "The School News," you will build fluency. When you read a script aloud,
- **say all the words correctly.**
- **slow down as needed** to read accurately.

Comprehension Strategies

As you read "I Live in a Town," you will review the two comprehension strategies you learned in Theme 1.
- **Use Graphic Organizers** Use a graphic organizer to help you organize what you already know and what you learn.

K	W	L
What I **Know**	What I **Want** to Know	What I **Learned**

- **Use Prior Knowledge** Use what you already know to help you understand what you read.

Writing

In Theme 1, you wrote several things. In Lesson 5, you will choose one piece of writing to revise and publish.

Tip

Writing Traits Think about how you can use ideas and organization to make your writing better.

SAMPLE REVISION

Look at how the paragraph below was revised. What makes the revised paragraph better?

There were many clouds. I looked up in the sky last night. It was raining. I could see a lot of lightning.

I looked up in the sky last night. It was raining. The dark black clouds filled the sky. I could see lightning everywhere.

Background and Vocabulary

Selections You Will Read
- "The Babe & I"
- "America's National Pastime"

"The Babe & I" is **historical fiction**.
Historical Fiction
- happens at a real time and place in the past
- has facts as well as opinions about people in history

What is "The Babe & I" about?

In this story, a boy sells newspapers to help his family. He meets a famous baseball player.

game of ▶
baseball

The **game of baseball** is played with nine people. They hit a ball with a bat and then run around the bases.

People who play the game are called **baseball players**. Babe Ruth was a famous player from the past.

baseball ▶
player

What vocabulary will you learn?

Robust Vocabulary

shabby

embarrass

midst

elevated

dazed

collapses

Tip

As you learn new words, remember to write them in your Vocabulary Log. Which words do you know very well? Which words are you still learning?

Word Bank

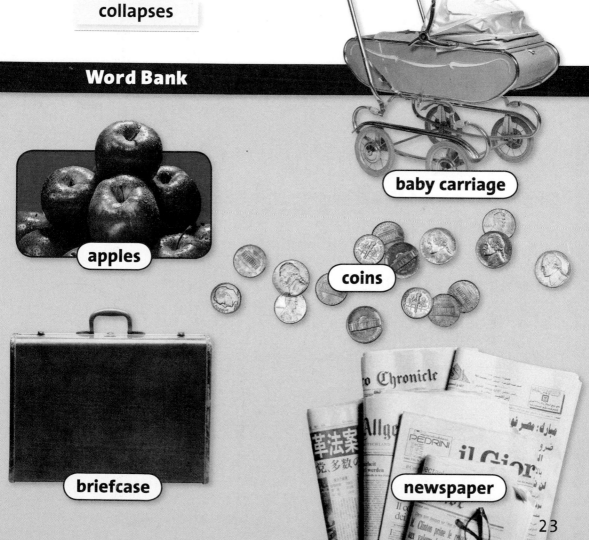

baby carriage

apples

coins

briefcase

newspaper

Phonics and Spelling

Look at these words.

Each word is a **compound word**. A **compound word** is a word made up of two or more smaller words. You can use the meanings of the smaller words to figure out what the **compound word** means.

stoplight	sandbox	newspaper

Read the words aloud. Look for the two smaller words in each compound word.

football ▶

◀ backpack

Grammar and Writing

What is the grammar skill?

You will learn about **simple and compound sentences.** A **simple sentence** tells a complete thought. A **compound sentence** is two sentences put together to make one new sentence.

Sentences can be put together using the words *and, but,* or *or.*

Mike plays soccer, and Jim plays baseball.

↑
compound sentence

Comprehension

What is the focus skill in this lesson?

The focus skill is **Fact and Opinion.** Knowing the difference between facts and opinions helps you make judgments about the selection.

To understand fact and opinion, remember:

- A **fact** is a statement that you can prove. You can check to make sure that it is true.
- An **opinion** is how someone thinks or feels about something. It cannot be proved to be true.

Read the passage.

Last night, we watched the sunset at 8:15 p.m. It was a beautiful sight. The sky became yellow and orange. It was the best sunset ever!

Sentences 1 and 3 tell facts. Sentences 2 and 4 tell opinions.

Background and Vocabulary

Selections You Will Read

- "Aero and Officer Mike"
- "It's All About Dogs"

"Aero and Officer Mike" is **nonfiction**.
Nonfiction

- has information about real people, real animals, or real events
- has facts about the topic and opinions the author may have

What is "Aero and Officer Mike" about?

This selection is about a dog that is trained to work with the police. Aero is a police dog.

A **police dog** helps a **police officer** do his or her job of keeping people safe.

police officer and ▶
police dog

What vocabulary will you learn?

Robust Vocabulary

scent

wanders

whined

obey

demonstrate

patrol

Tip

Remember to look in the Glossary for explantions of the words. What other strategies can you use?

badge

Word Bank

obstacle course

tennis ball

remote control

veterinarian

Phonics and Spelling

Sometimes two or three **consonants** are written together to make a new sound.

Consonant Pattern	Example
-tch, -ch	patch, touch
-sh, -ch	ship, machine
wh-	when

Read these words aloud. Listen to the sound of the consonants.

pitch **rich** **where**

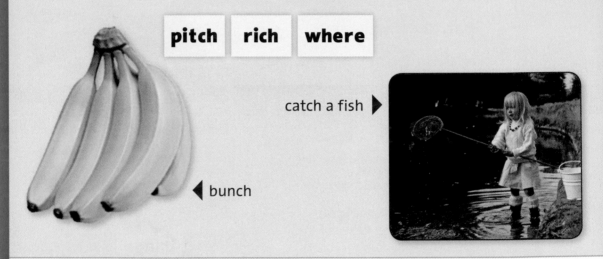

catch a fish ▶

◀ bunch

Grammar and Writing

What is the grammar skill?

You will learn about **common** and **proper nouns**. A **common noun** is any person, place, or thing. **Proper nouns** are special people, places, or things. Use a capital letter to show a **proper noun.**

Mrs. Willis is a teacher.

proper noun   common noun

28

Comprehension

What is the focus skill in this lesson?

The focus skill is **Fact and Opinion.** A fact is a statement that you can prove to be true. An opinion is the way someone thinks or feels.

To tell if a statement is an opinion:
• Ask, "Is this what one person thinks or believes?"

Read the passage.

> Nadia and Lisa have a cocker spaniel. It is light brown. They feed it and take it for walks. Cocker spaniels make the best pets.

The first three sentences are facts. The last sentence is an opinion.

29

Background and Vocabulary

Selections You Will Read
- "How Animals Talk"
- "Partners in the Wild"

"How Animals Talk" is a **photo essay**.
A Photo Essay
- has photographs that are supported by the text
- has paragraphs of information with details that support the main idea

What is "How Animals Talk" about?

This selection is about many different ways that animals talk to each other and share information.

Communicate means to share information or tell things. People often communicate with words. We also communicate with our bodies.

communicate ▼

What vocabulary will you learn?

Robust Vocabulary

signal

flick

alert

communicate

chatter

grooms

Tip

As you learn new words, remember to write them in your Vocabulary Log. Which words do you know very well? Which words are you still learning?

Word Bank

spider web

stream

branch

wings

horns

Phonics and Spelling

The /ou/ sound can be spelled *ow* as in *how* or *ou* as in *loud*.
The /oi/ sound can be spelled *oi* as in *foil* or *oy* as in *boy*.

how	loud	foil	toy

Read the words aloud. Listen for the vowel sound.

▼ mouse

◄ cowboy

Grammar and Writing

What is the grammar skill?

You will learn about **abbreviations**. **Abbreviations** are a shorter way of writing a word.

Elm St.   Dr. Anita Jones

abbreviation

Comprehension

What is the focus skill in this lesson?

The focus skill is **Main Idea and Details.** Good readers look for the main idea, which is the most important idea. Then, they look for details that support the main idea.

To understand the main idea and details:

• look for the most important idea in the paragraph or story
• then, look for details that tell about the main idea

Read the passage.

> Forests are a good place for bobcats to live. They make their homes in hollow trees. They survive by eating rabbits, squirrels, and birds that live in the forest, too.

The main idea: Forests are a good place for bobcats to live. Details: They make their homes in hollow trees. They survive by eating rabbits, squirrels, and birds that live in the forest, too.

33

Background and Vocabulary

Selections You Will Read

- "Stone Soup"
- "The Legend of Johnny Appleseed"

"Stone Soup" is a **folktale**. Folktales
- have events that repeat
- have story details that come together
  to teach a lesson

What is "Stone Soup" about?

This story is about villagers who learn that they
are happier when they share with each other.

Soup is a kind of food made of liquid and other foods.
You can add many different things to soup. Adding
more foods makes the soup taste better.

A **stone** is another name for a rock.

soup ▼

stone ▼

What vocabulary will you learn?

Robust Vocabulary

generous

banquet

gaze

agreeable

curiosity

famine

ingredients

momentum

Tip

Be a Word Detective! Look for these words in newspapers, magazines, and books. Listen for the words on the radio or television.

Word Bank

onions

mushrooms

window

carrots

pot

35

Phonics and Spelling

Some words have **consonants** that we blend together. We can hear each of the consonant sounds when we say the words.

strike	scratch	spray

Read the words aloud. Listen for the consonant blends.

◀ spring

stripe ▶

Grammar and Writing

What is the grammar skill?

You will learn about **singular** and **plural nouns**. A **singular noun** names one person, place, or thing. A **plural noun** names more than one person, place, or thing.

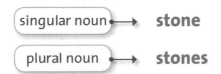

singular noun ⟶ **stone**

plural noun ⟶ **stones**

Comprehension

What is the focus skill in this lesson?

The focus skill is **Main Idea and Details.** The **main idea** is the most important idea in the story. **Details** give more information about the main idea.

To understand the main idea and details:

- try looking for the main idea at the beginning and the ending of the story
- look at the details of the story's problem and solution to see what they tell you about the main idea

Read the passage.

My favorite place in town is the park. The big, old trees are beautiful in every season. The soccer field is always full of excitement. Most of all, I love the playground.

The main idea is in the first sentence. The other sentences give details about the main idea.

Background and Vocabulary

Selections You Will Read

You will read a story titled "The Case of the Three Bears' Breakfast." The story is a **Readers' Theater.**

READERS' THEATER

COMPREHENSION STRATEGIES

You will also read a selection titled "How Living Things Survive." It is **nonfiction**. Nonfiction is writing that tells true facts or events.

What are the selections about?

"The Case of the Three Bears' Breakfast" is a mystery about who ate the bears' breakfast and made a mess of their house.

"How Living Things Survive" tells how some animals and plants change in order to keep living.

◀ A detective looks for clues to figure out how to solve a problem.

▼ The horned chameleon changes color to blend with its surroundings.

What vocabulary will you learn?

Robust Vocabulary

investigate

expert

laboratory

various

suspect

confess

Tip

As you learn new words, remember to write them in your Vocabulary Log. Which words do you know very well? Which words are you still learning?

Word Bank

bear

banana

chair

pancakes

crumbs

Fluency

As you read "The Case of the Three Bears' Breakfast," you will build fluency. When you read a script aloud,

- **group words that go together** to read naturally.
- **use punctuation** to help you read your character's lines with expression.

Comprehension Strategies

As you read "How Living Things Survive," you will review the two comprehension strategies you learned in Theme 2.

- **Monitor Comprehension—Reread** Reread to monitor comprehension and better understand what you have read.
- **Summarize** Summarize after reading a paragraph, a section of text, or the complete lesson. Do this to remember the most important ideas.

Main Idea		
Detail	Detail	Detail

Writing

In Theme 2, you wrote several things. In Lesson 10, you will choose one piece of writing to revise and publish.

> **Tip**
> **Writing Traits** Think about how **sentence fluency** and **word choice** can make your writing better.

Look at how the paragraph below was revised. What makes the revised paragraph better?

Gina plays piano. She has played for two years. She likes it. She knows many songs. She is good.

Gina plays piano. She has played for two years, and she likes it very much. Gina knows many songs and is a wonderful musician.

Lesson 11

Background and Vocabulary

Selections You Will Read

- "Loved Best"
- "The Shepherd Boy and the Wolf"

"Loved Best" is **realistic fiction**. Realistic Fiction

- has characters who behave as real people might behave
- has problems that are similar to problems in real life

What is "Loved Best" about?

This story is about a girl named Carolyn. When Carolyn performs in a play, she learns that her parents love all their children the same.

Carolyn forgot her lines while she was **performing** in the play.

What vocabulary will you learn?

encouraging

brief

chuckling

soothing

sobbed

praised

envious

rivalry

Tip

Remember to look in the Glossary for explanations of the words. What other strategies can you use?

Word Bank

bee

river

microphone

sunflower

43

Phonics and Spelling

When a word has **double consonants** in the middle, followed by the letters -*le*, the word is divided into syllables between the double consonants.

Word	Syllables
middle	mid/dle
apple	ap/ple
little	lit/tle

uncle   **rattle**

Read each word aloud. Notice that the words are divided into syllables between the double consonants.

Read these words.

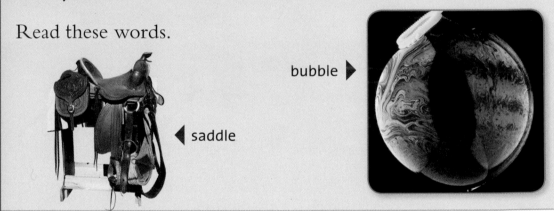

bubble ▶

◀ saddle

Grammar and Writing

What is the grammar skill?

You will learn about **possessive nouns.** Possessive nouns are formed by adding *'s* to a noun.

I stand next to the teacher's desk.

possessive noun

Comprehension

What is the focus skill in this lesson?

The focus skill is **Plot**. The plot is what happens in a story.

To understand the plot:
- think about the story's main problem and how it is solved
- look for important events

Read the passage.

Veronica is worried about her test on Friday. Her grandfather tells her to study every day. He even offers to help Veronica study. Each night the two work very hard. On Friday, Veronica is ready to take the test. She passes!

The plot is that Veronica studies for a test.

Background and Vocabulary

Selections You Will Read

- "A Pen Pal for Max"
- "Postcards from Around the World"

"A Pen Pal for Max" is **realistic fiction**.
Realistic fiction

- has characters with problems people might face in real life
- has a setting that could be real

What is "A Pen Pal for Max" about?

This story is about a boy named Max who lives in Chile. Max becomes pen pals with a girl who lives in the United States.

Max lives in South America. His **pen pal** lives in the United States.

◀ pen pal

What vocabulary will you learn?

Robust Vocabulary

translate

repairs

heaving

bothersome

din

dodging

catastrophe

fortunate

Tip

As you learn new words, remember to write them in your Vocabulary Log. Which words do you know very well? Which words are you still learning?

grapes

Word Bank

letter

pony

stamp

vineyard

47

Phonics and Spelling

Some words have a silent first letter. The *kn-* in the word *knot* is pronounced /n/. The *gn-* of *gnat* is pronounced /n/. The *wr-* of *wrist* is pronounced /r/.

knee   gnat   wrist

Read the words aloud. Each of these words has a silent first letter.

wrench ▶

▲ knot

Grammar and Writing

What is the grammar skill?

You will learn about **pronouns.** Pronouns are words that take the place of nouns.

I explained the exercise to the girl.

I explained the exercise to her.

pronoun

48

Comprehension

What is the focus skill in this lesson?

The focus skill is **Plot**. The plot is what happens in a story.

To understand the plot:
- find the problem in a story
- think about how the characters solve the problem

Read the passage.

Leah found a baby bird on the ground. She decided to ask her father for help. Her father found a nest in a nearby tree. He placed that baby bird in the nest. The two other baby birds chirped loudly. They were glad to have their brother back.

The plot is that Leah and her father helped the baby bird get home.

Background and Vocabulary

Selections You Will Read
- "A Tree Is Growing"
- "Ancient Trees Survive"

"A Tree Is Growing" is **expository nonfiction**. Expository nonfiction
- has facts and details that help explain the subject
- uses illustrations and captions

What is "A Tree Is Growing" about?

This selection explains what trees need to grow and how they grow. It also tells how the climate can change the way trees look.

buds in the spring ▶

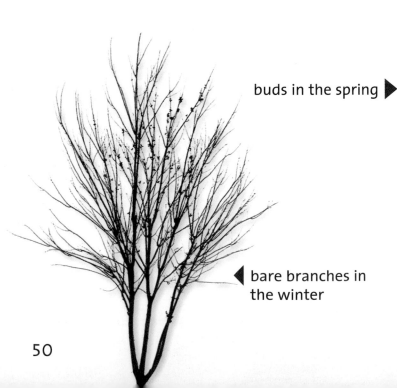

◀ bare branches in the winter

50

What vocabulary will you learn?

Robust Vocabulary

- columns
- absorb
- protects
- rustling
- dissolve
- particles
- scavenger
- self-sufficient

Tip

Be a Word Detective! Look for these words in newspapers, magazines, and books. Listen for the words on the radio or television.

Word Bank

roots

ring

trunk

acorns

mushrooms

51

Phonics and Spelling

The letters *c* and *g* can have different sounds. The *c* can have the /k/ or /s/ sound. The *g* can have /g/ or /j/ sound.

cat	cereal	game	giant

Read the words aloud. Notice the sound of *c* and *g*.

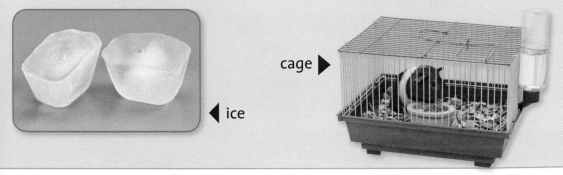

◀ ice

cage ▶

Grammar and Writing

What is the grammar skill?

You will learn about **subject pronouns.** Subject pronouns replace the subject in a sentence.

Leaves may turn red in autumn.

They may also turn yellow or orange.

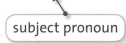

subject pronoun

Comprehension

What is the focus skill in this lesson?

The focus skill is **Author's Purpose.**

The author's purpose in expository nonfiction is to inform the reader about a topic.

To understand the author's purpose:
- think about the author's main message
- think about why the author wants to give this message

Read the passage.

> Pine trees have a special kind of leaves called pine needles. Pine cones grow on pine trees. Pine trees also have a special smell that many people like.

The author's purpose is to tell you about pine trees.

Background and Vocabulary

Selections You Will Read
- "One Small Place in a Tree"
- "Be a Bird Watcher"

"One Small Place in a Tree" is **expository nonfiction**. Expository nonfiction

- explains information and ideas
- has illustrations and details to help you learn about a topic

What is "One Small Place in a Tree" about?

This selection tells about one small hole in a tree, which was made by a bear's claws. The hole can be a home for many living things.

Black bears sharpen ▶
their **claws** on trees.

What vocabulary will you learn?

Robust Vocabulary

- suppose
- roost
- spears
- strikes
- glimpse
- maze

Tip

Be a Word Detective! Look for these words in newspapers, magazines, and books. Listen for the words on the radio or television.

Word Bank

snake

bluebird

bark

woodpecker

flying squirrel

Phonics and Spelling

Words that have two syllables and end in **-er** can have a long vowel sound or a short vowel sound.

music	river

Read the words aloud. Both words have two syllables. Both words end in *-er*.

tiger ▶

◀ robin

Grammar and Writing

What is the grammar skill?

You will learn about **pronoun–antecedent agreement.** Pronouns and the nouns that come before must have the same gender.

The <u>girl</u> took a picture with <u>her</u> camera.

Comprehension

What is the focus skill in this lesson?

The focus skill is **Author's Purpose.** An author's purpose in writing a story is to inform, entertain, or persuade. Knowing an author's purpose helps you understand the text.

To understand the author's purpose:

• look for clues in the text
• think about why the author thought the information in the text was important

Read the passage.

> Birds have wings that help them fly through the air. Some birds have feet that help them stand on branches. Others have feet to help them swim. Birds also have beaks. Their beaks are shaped to help them eat different types of food.

Here, the author's purpose is to give information about birds.

Background and Vocabulary

Selections You Will Read

You will read a selection titled "Ask the Experts." The selection is a **Readers' Theater.**

READERS' THEATER

You will also read a story titled "Iris and Walter, True Friends." This story is from a **chapter book**. A chapter book is a long story divided into smaller sections called chapters.

COMPREHENSION STRATEGIES

What are the selections about?

"Ask the Experts" tells about a group of students who work together to produce a student advice magazine.

"Iris and Walter, True Friends" tells how a boy teaches his friend about patience in getting something that she really wants.

▼ students working together

What vocabulary will you learn?

Robust Vocabulary

issue

advice

consult

recommend

sensible

devise

Tip

Use the Glossary to learn what a word means. The Glossary is found at the back of your book.

Word Bank

magazines

laptop

running

jumping

As you read "Ask the Experts," you will build fluency. When you read a script aloud,

- **read with feeling**, the way a person would speak.
- **let your voice rise and fall naturally** to show the character's feelings.

Comprehension Strategies

As you read "Iris and Walter, True Friends," you will review the two comprehension strategies you learned in Theme 3.

- **Use Story Structure** Use what you know about how stories are arranged to help you understand a chapter book.
- **Ask Questions** Ask yourself questions before, while, and after you read.

	Chapter 1	Chapter 2
What is happening in this chapter?		
How do the characters behave?		
What will happen next?		

Writing

In Theme 3, you wrote several things. In Lesson 15, you will choose one piece of writing to revise and publish.

> **Tip**
> **Writing Traits** Think about how you can use **voice** and **sentence fluency** to make your writing better.

SAMPLE REVISION

Look at how the paragraph below was revised. What makes the revised paragraph better?

I need a book. I will ask Mr. Robles. I can read on vacation. It will be fun.

I would like to bring a book on my vacation. I will ask Mr. Robles to help me choose one. He works in the library at school. I know he will help me find something fun to read on my trip.

Background and Vocabulary

Selections You Will Read

- "Lon Po Po"
- "Abuelita's Lap"

"Lon Po Po" is a **fairy tale**. Fairy tales

- are stories that take place in a make-believe world
- have a character who tries to outsmart children
- have a character who is clever and courageous

What is "Lon Po Po" about?

This selection is about a wolf who tries to trick children into thinking he is their grandmother.

A **wolf** is a wild animal that looks like a dog.

▼ wolf

What vocabulary will you learn?

tender

delighted

brittle

embraced

cunning

disguised

Tip

Be a Word Detective! Look for these words in newspapers, magazines, and books. Listen for the words on the radio or television.

rope

Word Bank

candle

claws

thorns

basket

Phonics and Spelling

Words with the **/ôr/ sound** can be spelled in many ways.

your	story	warn

Read the words aloud. Each word has the /ôr/ sound.

◄ shore

door ▶

Grammar and Writing

What is the grammar skill?

You will learn about **adjectives.** Adjectives tell about nouns. Many adjectives tell what kind.

The brown wolf sat in the snow.

Adjective

Comprehension

What is the focus skill in this lesson?

The focus skill is **Compare and Contrast**. To compare means to tell how things are the same. To contrast means to tell how things are different.

To understand compare and contrast:

• choose two people or things
• think about how they are the same and how they are different

Read the passage.

Sam and Maria each went on a trip. Sam went to ski in the mountains. He loved being in the snow. Maria went swimming at the beach. She played in the sand. Both Sam and Maria had fun.

When you compare, you see that Sam and Maria both went on trips. They both had fun outside. When you contrast, you see that Sam went to the snowy mountains. Maria went to the sandy beach.

Maria's trip ▶

◀ Sam's trip

65

Background and Vocabulary

Selections You Will Read
- "Two Bear Cubs"
- "Brave Measuring Worm"

"Two Bear Cubs" is a **play.** A play
- is a story that can be performed for an audience
- has parts that are read and acted out by performers
- has characters that may be alike in some ways but very different in others.

What is "Two Bear Cubs" about?

This play is about a small worm that saves two bear cubs that are in trouble.

Baby bears are called **cubs.**

A **mountain** is a very high hill.

mother bear and cubs ▶

▼ mountain

What vocabulary will you learn?

Robust Vocabulary

- glancing
- scolding
- console
- heroic
- drowsy
- burden

Tip

As you learn new words, remember to write them in your Vocabulary Log. Which words do you know very well? Which words are you still learning?

Word Bank

fox

hawk

mouse

caterpillar

deer

67

Phonics and Spelling

Words with the **/ûr/ sound** are spelled in different ways.

twirl	turn	work	heard	her

Read the words aloud. Each word has the /ûr/ sound.

Here is another word with the sound /ûr/. Read the word.

purse ▶

Grammar and Writing

What is the grammar skill?

You will learn about **adjectives that compare**. Some adjectives are used to compare two or more nouns.

Matt is the tallest in the group.

adjective that compares

Comprehension

What is the focus skill in this lesson?

The focus skill is **Compare and Contrast**. You compare by thinking about how things are alike. You contrast by thinking about how things are different.

To understand comparing and contrasting:

- think about how the characters act the same or differently
- notice how the characters change from the beginning to the end of the story

Read the passage.

> Kara and Tim both like to play sports. Kara plays baseball. Her team won first place last year. Tim plays basketball. He scored ten points in his last game. Kara and Tim are good friends, but they like to play different kinds of games.

When you compare Kara and Tim, you see they are alike because they both like to play sports. When you contrast them, you see that they are different because one plays baseball and the other plays basketball.

69

Background and Vocabulary

Selections You Will Read

- "Me and Uncle Romie"
- "The Art of Collage"

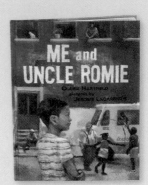

"Me and Uncle Romie" is historical fiction.
Historical fiction

- has people and places that are real or could be real
- has events that did happen or could have happened

What is "Me and Uncle Romie" about?

This selection is about a boy named James from a quiet part of North Carolina. He visits his aunt and uncle in New York City.

▼ New York City

What vocabulary will you learn?

Robust Vocabulary

glorious

memory

ruined

streak

crept

yanked

fire hydrant

Word Bank

rooftop

apartment

fire escape

train

Phonics and Spelling

A **suffix** is a word part that can be added to the end of a word. Adding a suffix changes the meaning of a word.

Read the words aloud. Each word has a suffix.

Word	Suffix	Meaning
teacher	-er	a person who
sharpest	-est	most
slowly	-ly	the way something is done
hopeful	-ful	full of

The girl walks slowly. ▶

Grammar and Writing
What is the grammar skill?

You will learn about **articles.** An article is a short word. It tells about a person, place, or thing. *The, an,* and *a* are articles.

Use *a* before a word that starts with a consonant. Use *an* before a word that starts with a vowel.

I read a book about an elephant.

article   article

Comprehension

What is the focus skill in this lesson?

The focus skill is **Theme.** The theme is the message or idea about life that the author wants the reader to understand.

To understand the theme:
- notice what the characters say and do
- think about the author's message to you

Read the passage.

> Lisa's family is moving out of town. This is Lisa's last day of school. Alex and Andrea want Lisa to know that they care. They take pictures of everyone in the class. They make a book that Lisa can take with her.

The theme is "Friends can help someone feel better by making something special."

Background and Vocabulary

Selections You Will Read

- "Half Chicken"
- "I Sailed on Half a Ship"

"Half Chicken" is a **folktale**. Folktales
- are stories that have been passed down through time
- sometimes explain how something came to be
- may have a theme that teaches a lesson

What is "Half Chicken" about?

This selection explains why some weather vanes have roosters at their top.

A **weather vane** shows the direction of the wind.

A **rooster** is a male chicken.

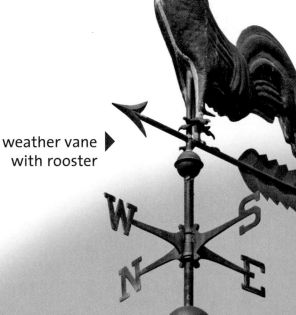

weather vane ▶
with rooster

What vocabulary will you learn?

Robust Vocabulary

swift

vain

overheard

suggested

enormous

exclaimed

Tip

Be a Word Detective! Look for these words in newspapers, magazines, and books. Listen for the words on the radio or television.

Word Bank

stream

kettle

calves

Phonics and Spelling

A **prefix** is a word part that can be added to the beginning of a word. Adding a prefix changes the meaning of a word.

undo	**reread**	**displeased**
un do	re read	dis pleased
"the opposite of do"	"read again"	"not pleased"

Read the words aloud. Each word has a prefix.

I can rewrite my spelling words. ▶

Grammar and Writing
What is the grammar skill?

You will learn about **action verbs.** Action verbs tell what the subject does.

The rooster crows at dawn.

action verb

Comprehension

What is the focus skill in this lesson?

The focus skill is **Theme**. The theme is the message or idea about life that the author wants readers to understand.

To understand the theme:

• notice what the characters say and do
• think about the author's message to you

Read the passage.

> Herman the rooster awakes at dawn. He crows to wake the other animals on the farm. He soon sees the farmer step onto the front porch. The farmer arrives to feed the chickens. Herman smiles to himself as he starts to eat. Herman loves the start of a brand new day.

The theme is "Herman is proud that he has the job of starting the day for everyone."

77

Background and Vocabulary

Selections You Will Read

You will read a selection titled "Backstage with Chris and Casey." The selection is a **Readers' Theater**.

You will also read a selection titled "The Cracked Chinese Jug." This selection is a **fable**. Fables are brief stories that are used to teach valuable lessons.

What are the selections about?

"Backstage with Chris and Casey" tells about the people who put on plays. Each person has a different job.

"The Cracked Chinese Jug" tells about a clay water jug that has a crack. The jug feels useless because water leaks out of it.

▼ backstage at the theater

What vocabulary will you learn?

Robust Vocabulary

versions

rehearse

mandatory

criticize

immerse

dialogue

Tip

As you learn new words, remember to write them in your Vocabulary Log. Which words do you know very well? Which words are you still learning?

Word Bank

cast

designer

director

crew

Fluency

As you read "Backstage with Chris and Casey," you will build fluency. When you read a script aloud,

- **read carefully** so that you make as few mistakes as possible.
- **group words that go together** to make your reading sound natural.

Comprehension Strategies

As you read "The Cracked Chinese Jug," you will review the two comprehension strategies you learned in Theme 4.

- **Monitor Comprehension—Read Ahead** If you have trouble understanding what you have read, try reading ahead. You may find information that explains what was difficult to understand.
- **Use Story Structure** Use what you know about how stories are arranged to help you think about the characters, setting, problem, and solution of the story.

Characters		Setting
Problem		
Events		
Solution		
Theme		

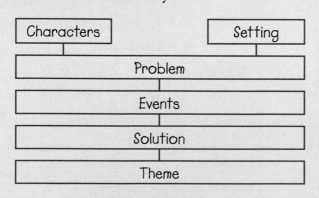

80

Writing

In Theme 4, you wrote several things. In Lesson 20, you will choose one piece of writing to revise and publish.

> **Tip**
> **Writing Traits** Think about how you can use **conventions** and **voice** to make your writing better.

SAMPLE REVISION

Look at how the paragraph below was revised. What makes the revised paragraph better?

> My name is rico. Tomorrow is my birthday. Let's go to the theater said my dad. i like this idea. I wonder if we can go backstage after the show.

> My name is Rico. Tomorrow is my birthday. "Let's go to the theater," said my dad. I like this idea. I wonder if we can go backstage after the show.

Background and Vocabulary

Selections You Will Read

- "Antarctic Ice"
- "Diary of a Very Short Winter Day"

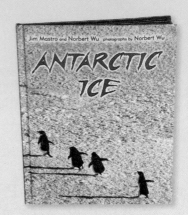

"Antarctic Ice" is **expository nonfiction**.
Expository nonfiction

- gives facts and details about a topic
- tells about events in time order

What is "Antarctic Ice" about?

This selection is about Antarctica, the coldest
place on Earth, and the animals that live there.

Antarctica is covered by ice.

This **penguin** and its baby live
in Antarctica.

ice ▶   penguin ▶

What vocabulary will you learn?

absence

shelters

permanently

drifts

scarce

dim

Tip

As you learn new words, remember to write them in your Vocabulary Log. Which words do you know very well? Which words are you still learning?

Word Bank

sun

microscope

climbs

ocean

Phonics and Spelling

The vowel sound /ü/ can be spelled with different letters: *oo, ew, ue, ui.*

Read the words aloud. Each word has the same vowel sound, /ü/.

new	blue	fruit	boot

fruit ▶

Grammar and Writing
What is the grammar skill?

You will learn about **the verb** *be.* Here are some forms of the verb *be.*

be verb
↓
I am going to school.

be verb
↓
She is going to school.

be verb
↓
They are going to school.

84

Comprehension

What is the focus skill in this lesson?

The focus skill is **Sequence.** Sequence is the order in which events happen.

To understand the sequence in a selection:

• look for words that give clues to the sequence. A few examples are *first, next, then, later,* and *finally.*

Read the passage.

First, Ben was a baby. Then, he learned to crawl. Next, he learned to walk and talk. He was a child. Now he is a big boy. He can skate on a skateboard.

The sequence tells the order in which Ben grew up.

85

Background and Vocabulary

Selections You Will Read
- "Bat Loves the Night"
- "Bottlenose Dolphins"

"Bat Loves the Night" is an **informational narrative**. Informational Narratives
- have facts about a topic
- tell events in time order

What is "Bat Loves the Night" about?
This selection is about a bat that hunts for food at night. She then returns home to take care of her babies.

A bat rests by hanging **upside down**.

A bat's **wing** is its hand and arm.

upside down ▶

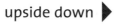

86

What vocabulary will you learn?

Robust Vocabulary

- nocturnal
- effort
- dozes
- swoops
- detail
- fluttering

Tip

Remember to look in the Glossary for explanations of the words. What other strategies can you use?

Word Bank

tree

fruit

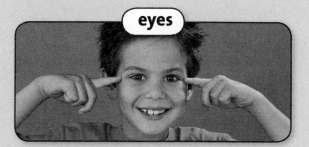

eyes

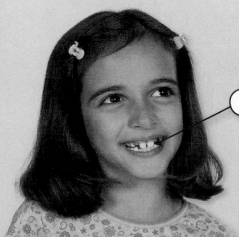

teeth

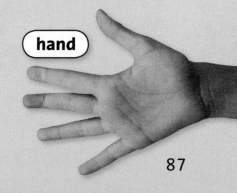

hand

87

Phonics and Spelling

The vowel sound /ô/ can be spelled with different letters. These are *au(gh)*, *aw*, *a(l)*, and *ough*.

| walk | straw | thought | taught |

Read the words aloud. Each word has the vowel sound /ô/.

yawn

Grammar and Writing

What is the grammar skill?

You will learn about **main and helping verbs**. The main verb tells the action. The helping verb tells whether the action takes place in the past, the present, or the future.

The bats have returned home.

helping verb   main verb

Comprehension

What is the focus skill in this lesson?

The focus skill is **Sequence**. The sequence is the order in which events happen.

To understand the sequence:

• look for words that help tell when something happened. Some of these are *during, while, until, before,* and *after.*

Read the passage.

> During my ride to school, the rain started. Just before the bus arrived at school, the rain stopped. After I got off the bus, I jumped in the puddles.

The sequence is the order of events during the girl's ride to school.

89

Background and Vocabulary

Selections You Will Read

- "Chestnut Cove"
- "Mayors"

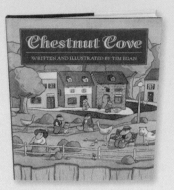

"Chestnut Cove" is a **fantasy**. In fantasies
- the characters may or may not be realistic
- something causes other events to happen

What is "Chestnut Cove" about?

This story is about people who get along well.
Things change when they compete to grow the
best watermelon.

A **watermelon** is a large fruit that is sweet
and juicy inside.

At **harvest** time, crops are ready to
be picked.

▼ watermelon

▼ the pear harvest

What vocabulary will you learn?

Robust Vocabulary

fondness

emotion

ridiculous

disgraceful

decent

inherit

Tip

Be a Word Detective! Look for these words in newspapers, magazines, and books. Listen for the words on the radio or television.

Word Bank

picnic

pig

cow

goat

castle

91

Phonics and Spelling

A **prefix** is a word part that can be added to the beginning of a word. Adding a prefix changes the meaning of a word.

Prefix	Meaning
in-	*not or the opposite of*
mis-	*bad, badly, wrongly*
pre-	*before or to go before*

Read the words aloud. Each word has a prefix.

incorrect	mismatch	preheat

These socks are ▲ mismatched.

Grammar and Writing

What is the grammar skill?

You will learn about **present-tense verbs.** A present-tense verb tells about an action that is happening now.

The people smile at each other.

↑ present-tense verb

92

Comprehension

What is the focus skill in this lesson?

The focus skill is **Cause and Effect.** The reason an event happens is the cause. What happens is the effect.

To find the cause, ask:
• Why did it happen?

To find the effect, ask:
• What happened?

Read the passage.

> I have a new baby brother. His name is Zane. He hasn't learned to talk yet, but he cries a lot. My mom says he cries to tell us things. Most of the time he cries because he is hungry.

The cause is that the baby is hungry. The effect is that the baby cries.

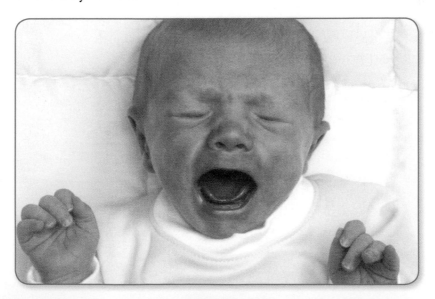

Background and Vocabulary

Selections You Will Read

- "Ramona Quimby, Age 8"
- "Slam Dunk Water"

"Ramona Quimby, Age 8" is **realistic fiction**. Realistic fiction

- has characters with realistic problems
- has cause-and-effect relationships like those in real life

What is "Ramona Quimby, Age 8" about?

This story is about a girl who prepares a book report for school. Then she forgets what she planned to say.

Homework is the schoolwork your teacher asks you to do at home.

A **book report** is what you have to say about a book you have read.

▲ book report

homework ▶

What vocabulary will you learn?

Robust Vocabulary

clutter

visible

mentioned

beckoned

flustered

remark

Word Bank

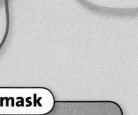

rubber bands

cat

mask

bus

95

Phonics and Spelling

When the schwa /ə/ sound is in the first syllable, the syllable is not stressed, or accented.

Read the words aloud. The schwa /ə/ sound is in the first syllable. This syllable is not stressed.

amount	afraid	applause

◀ applause

Grammar and Writing

What is the grammar skill?

You will learn about **past-tense** and **future-tense verbs.** A past-tense verb tells about an action that has already happened. Future-tense verbs tell about an action that is going to happen.

Last year, I learned to ride a bike.
⤒
past-tense verb

Next year, I will learn to skate.
⤒
future-tense verb

Comprehension

What is the focus skill in this lesson?

The focus skill is **Cause and Effect.** The reason an event happens is the cause. What happens is the effect.

To find the cause, ask:
• Why did it happen?

To find the effect, ask:
• What happened?

Read the passage.

> Ice freezes when the temperature is below freezing. When ice is taken out of a freezer and placed under a light, the ice starts to melt.

The bright light is causing the ice to melt. Melted ice is the effect.

Background and Vocabulary

Selections You Will Read

You will read a selection titled "The Robodogs of Greenville." The selection is a **Readers' Theater**.

READERS' THEATER

You will also read a selection titled "Fighting for Our Freedoms." This selection is **nonfiction**. Nonfiction is writing that tells true facts or events.

COMPREHENSION STRATEGIES

What are the selections about?

"The Robodogs of Greenville" tells about Earth in the year 2222, when dog robots have replaced real dogs.

"Fighting for Our Freedom" tells how the Thirteen Colonies began to fight to be free from England's control.

◀ A drummer boy marched with soldiers in the American Revolution.

robot ▶

What vocabulary will you learn?

Robust Vocabulary

required

functional

inhabitants

amazement

ample

responsibility

Tip

Be a Word Detective! Look for these words in newspapers, magazines, and books. Listen for the words on the radio or television.

Word Bank

chores

happy

pets

love

Fluency

As you read "The Robodogs of Greenville," you will build fluency. When you read a script aloud,

- **read at the same speed** at which you would speak to a friend.
- **use your voice** to express the way your character is feeling.

Comprehension Strategies

As you read "Fighting for Our Freedoms," you will review the two comprehension strategies you learned in Theme 5.

- **Reread** Monitor your comprehension each time you read. If something you are reading doesn't make sense the first time, try rereading it.
- **Answer Questions** Use information you have read to answer questions at the end of the sections. Look back in the text to check your answers.

Writing

In Theme 5, you wrote several things. In Lesson 25, you will choose one piece of writing to revise and publish.

Tip

Writing Traits ➤ Think about how you can use **sentence fluency** and **organization** to make your writing better.

SAMPLE REVISION

Look at how the paragraph below was revised. What makes the revised paragraph better?

> People can work together. Chores get done faster. Two people can work in a garden. They can do more than one person.

> When people work together, chores get done faster. Three people can plant a garden quickly, and they can have fun together.

Background and Vocabulary

Selections You Will Read

- "Charlotte's Web"
- "Caterpillars Spin Webs, Too!"

"Charlotte's Web" is **fantasy**. Fantasy

- has characters, such as animals, that do things real animals cannot do
- has a plot with a beginning, middle, and end

What is "Charlotte's Web about?

"Charlotte's Web" tells of a friendship between a pig and a spider and what happens when the pig tries to spin a web.

Spiders spin **webs** with their legs.

Farm animals live in a **barn**.

web ▶

◀ barn

What vocabulary will you learn?

Robust Vocabulary

summoning

nuisance

sedentary

oblige

boasting

sway

Tip

Remember to look in the Glossary for explanations of the words. What other strategies can you use?

Word Bank

farm

friends

tail

bridge

103

Phonics and Spelling

Look at the endings of the words. Each word ends in either **-tion** or **-sion**. These word endings usually make the sound *shun*.

fiction	nation	vacation	discussion

Read the words aloud. Each word ends with the sound *shun*.

The students are having a **discussion**. ▶

◀ Some families **vacation** at the beach.

Grammar and Writing

What is the grammar skill?

You will learn about **irregular verbs**. **Irregular verbs** do not add *-ed* to form the past tense.

Luis has seen three rabbits in his yard.

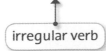

irregular verb

Comprehension

What is the focus skill in this lesson?

The focus skill is **Make Inferences**. A reader who makes inferences puts information together in order to understand what is happening.

To make inferences:
- think about what the author says
- think about what you know
- put the two together to get new information

Read the passage.

> Anna looked at the clock. She had five minutes before the bus came. She ran to the closet to grab her blue raincoat. She looked around the closet floor for her red umbrella. "Honk! Honk!" went the school bus. Anna was ready to go!

Anna needed a raincoat and umbrella. You can make an inference that it was raining outside.

Background and Vocabulary

Selections You Will Read

- "Spiders and Their Webs"
- "For You"

"Spiders and Their Webs" is **expository nonfiction**. Expository nonfiction

- gives facts and details about a topic
- might have charts that give additional information

What is "Spiders and Their Webs" about?

This selection is about different kinds of spiders and their webs.

▼ spider web

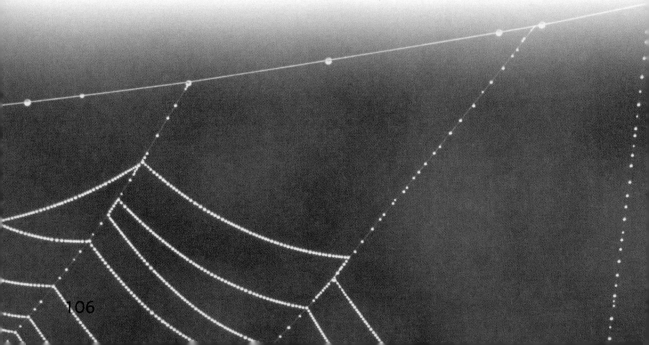

What vocabulary will you learn?

prey

shallow

strands

social

spiral

reels

Tip

As you learn new words, remember to write them in your Vocabulary Log. Which words do you know very well? Which words are you still learning?

bird

Word Bank

drink

build

plant

house

Phonics and Spelling

Sometimes two vowels together are in different syllables. The word is divided into syllables between the two vowels, as in *lion*.

Read the words aloud. Each word is divided into syllables between two vowels.

The **lion** sits in the sun. ▶

Grammar and Writing

What is the grammar skill?

You will learn about **adverbs**. Adverbs tell *how, when,* or *where.* The adverbs we usually use tell *how* we do something.

We walked to school slowly.

↑
adverb

Comprehension

What is the focus skill in this lesson?

The focus skill is **Make Inferences.** Good readers make inferences in order to figure out the missing information.

To make inferences:

- think about what the author says
- think about what you know
- put the two together to get new information

Read the passage.

> Ben and Sarah ran the race as hard as they could. They saw the finish line. Ben pushed his legs with every ounce of power he had. When his chest broke through the finish line, Ben was all smiles. Quickly Ben turned his head. Sarah was right behind him. She was smiling, too.

The author does not say that Ben won the race. You can make the inference from the other words in the story.

119

Background and Vocabulary

Selections You Will Read

- "The Science Fair"
- "Advice from Dr. Fix-It"

"The Science Fair" is **realistic fiction**.
Realistic fiction

- could happen in real life
- has details that help readers make predictions
- has a plot with a beginning, middle, and end

What is "The Science Fair" about?

This selection is about a girl and a boy who compete in a science fair.

At a science fair, students do **experiments**.

The **first place** blue ribbon goes to the best experiment.

▲ first place
blue ribbon

◀ experiment

What vocabulary will you learn?

Robust Vocabulary

sprinkled

expand

erupt

thorough

deliberation

grainy

Tip

Be a Word Detective! Look for these words in newspapers, magazines, and books. Listen for the words on the radio or television.

Word Bank

stars

fish bowl

bottle

volcano

Phonics and Spelling

A **suffix** is a word part that is added to the end of a word. Adding a suffix changes the meaning of a word.

| washable | flexible | helpless | dangerous | valuable |

Read the words aloud. Each word has a suffix.

valuable jewelry ▶

Grammar and Writing

What is the grammar skill?

You will learn about **subject pronoun contractions**. A subject pronoun tells who is the subject of a sentence. A contraction is two words shortened into one.

We'll take a rest from our hike.

↑

subject pronoun contraction

Comprehension

What is the focus skill in this lesson?

The focus skill is **Make Predictions**. Good readers make predictions about what might happen in a story.

To understand making predictions:

• pay attention to what is happening in the story
• look for clues that will help you make predictions about what could happen next

Read the passage.

> It took a lot of pushing and splashing, but Sonia and Julia finally got Cookie into the tub. Sonia held onto Cookie while Julia scrubbed the dog with soapy water. Cookie squirmed to the left and to the right. Sonia held on tight.

A reader could make the prediction that Cookie will run out of the tub when Sonia lets go of her.

Background and Vocabulary

Selections You Will Read

- "The Planets"
- "Jeremy's House"

"The Planets" is **expository nonfiction**.
Expository nonfiction

- explains information and ideas
- gives facts and details about a topic
- has captions and labels that tell about illustrations

What is "The Planets" about?

This selection is about the planets in our solar system.

Our solar system includes the **sun** and everything that circles it.

The **planets** circle the sun.

▼ the planets and the sun

What vocabulary will you learn?

Robust Vocabulary

rotates

surface

steady

reflects

appears

evidence

Tip

Remember to look in the Glossary for explanations of the words. What other strategies can you use?

Earth

Word Bank

river

clouds

Phonics and Spelling

A **prefix** is a word part that can be added to the beginning of a word. Adding a **prefix** changes the meaning of a word.

| bicycle | nonstop | overflow |

Prefix	Meaning
bi–	*twice; every other*
non–	*not, or lacking or without*
over–	*too or too much; covering or on top*

Read the words aloud. Each word has a prefix.

The boys are reading ▶ *non*fiction books.

◀ We heard the sound of a plane *over*head.

Grammar and Writing

What is the grammar skill?

You will learn about **capitalization**. Every sentence begins with a capital letter. Proper nouns also begin with capital letters.

The planets circle the sun.

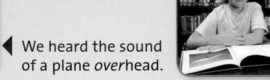

capital letter

Comprehension

What is the focus skill in this lesson?

The focus skill is **Make Predictions**. Readers make predictions when they think about what will happen next in a story.

To understand making predictions:
- think about what you have read
- look for clues about what will happen next

Read the passage.

> Brad opened his eyes. His bedroom was unusually bright. Why didn't his dad wake him up? Would he be late for school? Brad looked out the window. Snow was floating from the sky. The ground was covered with a white blanket of snow.

A reader can predict that Brad will find out that school is closed because of snow.

Background and Vocabulary

Selections You Will Read

You will read a selection titled "Voyage Across the Solar System." This selection is a **Readers' Theater**.

READERS' THEATER

You will also read a selection titled "Energy." This selection is **functional text**. Functional text is writing that is used by people every day. It is text that helps people answer questions and complete tasks.

COMPREHENSION STRATEGIES

What are the selections about?

"Voyage Across the Solar System" is a science fiction account of space travel to the planets.

In **"Energy,"** we learn that we cannot see energy, but we can see, hear, or feel its effects.

▼ energy from the sun

What vocabulary will you learn?

Robust Vocabulary

- magnify
- observed
- generates
- confirm
- picturesque
- safeguard

Tip

Use the Glossary to learn what a word means. The Glossary is found at the back of your book.

◀ spaceship

Word Bank

space suit

telescope

solar system

rings

119

Fluency

As you read "Voyage Across the Solar System," you will build fluency. When you read a script aloud,

- let your voice **rise and fall** as if you were speaking in a conversation.
- pay attention to the different kinds of **punctuation**

Comprehension Strategies

As you read "Energy," you will review the two comprehension strategies you learned in Theme 6.

- **Ask Questions** Ask yourself questions before, while, and after you read. What information are you after? What directions will you need to follow? What will the outcome be?
- **Read Ahead** Read ahead to see if new information is presented that explains something. When following directions, read ahead to find out what you will need and what you will do.

Writing

In Theme 6, you wrote several things. In Lesson 30, you will choose one piece of writing to revise and publish.

Tip

Writing Traits Think about how you can use **word choice** and **ideas** to make your writing better.

SAMPLE REVISION

Look at how the paragraph below was revised. What makes the revised paragraph better?

> Dr. Mae Jemison is a doctor. She also was an astronaut. She speaks different languages. Not many women went to space before her.

> Dr. Mae Jemison is a special person. She is a doctor who speaks four different languages. She was also the first African-American woman to go to space.

Using the Glossary

Like a dictionary, this glossary lists words in alphabetical order. To find a word, look it up by its first letter or letters.

To save time, use the guide words at the top of each page. These show the first and last words on the page. Look at the guide words to see if the word falls between them alphabetically.

Here is an example of a glossary entry:

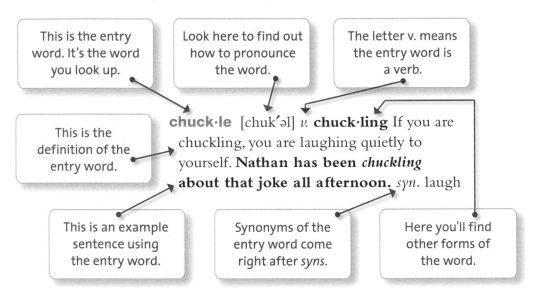

This is the entry word. It's the word you look up.

Look here to find out how to pronounce the word.

The letter v. means the entry word is a verb.

This is the definition of the entry word.

chuck·le [chuk'əl] *v.* **chuck·ling** If you are chuckling, you are laughing quietly to yourself. **Nathan has been *chuckling* about that joke all afternoon.** *syn.* laugh

This is an example sentence using the entry word.

Synonyms of the entry word come right after *syns*.

Here you'll find other forms of the word.

Word Origins

Throughout the glossary, you will find notes about word origins, or how words got started and have changed. Words often have interesting backgrounds that can help you remember what they mean.

Word Origins

uniform This word comes from the Latin word *uniformis*, meaning "one form." So if everyone wears only one form of clothing, they are wearing a uniform.

Pronunciation

The pronunciations in brackets are respellings that show how the words are pronounced. The **pronunciation** key explains what the symbols in a respelling mean. A shortened pronunciation key appears on every other page of the glossary.

PRONUNCIATION KEY

a	add, map	m	move, seem	u	up, done
ā	ace, rate	n	nice, tin	û(r)	burn, term
â(r)	care, air	ng	ring, song	yo͞o	fuse, few
ä	palm, father	o	odd, hot	v	vain, eve
b	bat, rub	ō	open, so	w	win, away
ch	check, catch	ô	order, jaw	y	yet, yearn
d	dog, rod	oi	oil, boy	z	zest, muse
e	end, pet	ou	pout, now	zh	vision, pleasure
ē	equal, tree	o͝o	took, full	ə	the schwa, an
f	fit, half	o͞o	pool, food		unstressed vowel
g	go, log	p	pit, stop		representing the
h	hope, hat	r	run, poor		sound spelled
i	it, give	s	see, pass		a in above
ī	ice, write	sh	sure, rush		e in sicken
j	joy, ledge	t	talk, sit		i in possible
k	cool, take	th	thin, both		o in melon
l	look, rule	th	this, bathe		u in circus

Other symbols:
- • separates words into syllables
- ´ indicates heavier stress on a syllable
- ´ indicates lighter stress on a syllable

Abbreviations: *adj.* adjective, *adv.* adverb, *conj.* conjunction, *interj.* interjection, *n.* noun, *prep.* preposition, *pron.* pronoun, *syn.* synonym, *v.* verb

A

ab·sence [ab′səns] *n.* Absence means that something or someone is not present. **There was an *absence* of fresh water on the island.** *syn.* lack

ab·sorb [əb·zôrb′] *v.* Something absorbs a liquid if it soaks up the liquid. **The towel will *absorb* the water.** *syn.* take in

> **ACADEMIC LANGUAGE**
>
> **accuracy** When you read with *accuracy,* you read without any mistakes.
>
> **advertisement** An *advertisement* is written to sell a product or tell about an event.

ad·vice [ad·vīs′] *n.* If you give someone advice, you tell what you think the person should do. **Lauren's *advice* was to choose the game that was the most fun to play.** *syn.* recommendation

> **ACADEMIC LANGUAGE**
>
> **advice column** An *advice column* gives suggestions for how to solve a problem, and is found in a newspaper or magazine.

a·gree·a·ble [ə·grē′ə·bəl] *adj.* Something that is agreeable is pleasing to the senses. **The smell of an apple pie baking was very *agreeable.*** *syn.* pleasant

a·lert [ə·lûrt′] *v.* If you alert people to something, you get their attention and let them know to be careful. **The smoke alarm will *alert* you to the fact that fire is present.** *syn.* notify

a·maze·ment [ə·māz′mənt] *n.* Amazement is a feeling of great wonder and surprise. **When Destinee's baby brother said his first words, she gasped in *amazement.*** *syn.* surprise

am·ple [am′pəl] *adj.* An amount that is ample is enough or more than is needed. **The boys had *ample* space to play football in the yard.** *syns.* enough, plenty

ap·pear [ə·pir′] *v.* ap·pears How something appears is the way it looks or seems to be. **Jacob *appears* to be unhappy.** *syn.* seem

ap·ply [ə·plī′] *v.* When you apply for a job, you are asking for work. **Kiarra will call the company to *apply* for a job.** *syns.* request, ask

as·sem·bly [ə·sem′blē] *n.* An assembly is a group of people who have gathered for a reason. **The school will hold an *assembly* to honor the reading contest winners.** *syns.* meeting, gathering

au·to·graph [ô′tə·graf′] *v.* **au·to·graphed** If you autographed something, you signed your name on it.

autograph

Adam's friends *autographed* his yearbook. *syn.* sign

B

ban·quet [bang′kwit] *n.* If you are going to a banquet, you are going to a special meal that will have a large amount of food. **There will be a lot of food at the *banquet*.** *syn.* feast

banquet

beck·on [bek′ən] *v.* **beck·oned** If you beckoned to someone, you used your hand to signal him or her to come to you. **Alyssa *beckoned* to Daisy to come over to her desk.** *syn.* summon

boast [bōst] *v.* **boast·ing** Someone who is boasting is telling other people wonderful things about himself or herself. **Joseph was always *boasting* about how fast he could run.** *syn.* brag

both·er·some [both′ər·səm] *adj.* When something is bothersome, it bothers you and causes problems. **The broken zipper on my boot is *bothersome*!** *syn.* annoying

brief [brēf] *adj.* If something is brief, it does not take much time. **The class will take a *brief* break before continuing the test.** *syn.* short

a	add	e	end	o	odd	ōō	pool	oi	oil	th	this		*a* in *above*
ā	ace	ē	equal	ō	open	u	up	ou	pout	zh	vision		*e* in *sicken*
â	care	i	it	ô	order	û	burn	ng	ring			ə =	*i* in *possible*
ä	palm	ī	ice	ōō	took	yōō	fuse	th	thin				*o* in *melon*
													u in *circus*

brit·tle [brit′əl] *adj.* Things that are brittle are so stiff and hard that they break easily. **A glass vase can be easily broken because it is** *brittle.* *syns.* fragile, breakable

bur·den [bûr′dən] *n.* A burden is a heavy load that is difficult to carry. **For Sierra, the stack of books was a heavy** *burden.*

cam·ou·flage [kam′ə·fläzh′] *n.* When something has camouflage, it blends into its surroundings. **An arctic hare has white fur in winter as** *camouflage* **against the snow.**

--- **Word Origins** ---

camouflage *Camouflage* comes from the Italian *camuffare,* which means "disguise or trick." This word got its start during World War I, when soldiers practiced hiding objects from the enemy.

cer·tain [sûr′tən] *adj.* A certain thing is one particular thing. **Cole wants a** *certain* **kind of candy.** *syn.* specific

chat·ter [chat′ər] *v.* When animals chatter, they repeat their sounds quickly. **I heard the squirrels** *chatter* **outside.** *syn.* talk

chore [chôr] *n.* **chores** Chores are small jobs that you need to do but may not enjoy. **Julia has to do her** *chores* **at home every day.** *syn.* duty

chuck·le [chuk′əl] *v.* **chuck·ling** If you are chuckling, you are laughing quietly to yourself. **Nathan has been** *chuckling* **about that joke all afternoon.** *syn.* laugh

clut·ter [klut′ər] *n.* If a place such as your desk or your room has clutter, it is messy and full of things you do not really need. **The floor of the playroom was covered with** *clutter.*

co·in·ci·dence [kō·in′sə·dəns] *n.* A coincidence is when two things happen that seem to fit together but are not connected. **It was a** *coincidence* **that Sophia and Mackenzie wore identical shirts today.**

col·lapse [kə·laps′] *v.* **col·lap·ses** When something collapses, it falls down because it is not well supported. **"Run out of the tent before it collapses!" I yelled.**

col·umn [kol′əm] *n.* **col·umns** A column is a tall, circular structure that holds up part of a building. **The roof of the porch is held up by** *columns.* *syn.* pole

column

com·mu·ni·cate [kə·myoo′nə·kāt′] *v.* When two people or animals communicate, they share information. **One way people** *communicate* **is by talking.**

--- Word Origins ---

communicate *Communicate* comes from the Latin *communicatus,* which means "share."

con·ceal [kən·sēl′] *v.* **con·cealed** Something that is concealed is covered up so it can't be seen. **Malik wanted to surprise his dad, so he** *concealed* **the gift under the couch.** *syn.* hide

con·fess [kən·fes′] *v.* When you confess, you tell the truth about something you did wrong. **It can be hard to** *confess* **that you have made a mistake, but it is best to tell the truth.** *syn.* admit

con·firm [kən·fûrm′] *v.* When you can prove something is correct, you can confirm it. **The cashier called the store manager to** *confirm* **the price of the bananas.** *syn.* verify

con·sole [kən·sōl′] *v.* When you comfort or cheer someone, you console him or her. **My friends tried to** *console* **me after I lost the race.** *syn.* encourage

con·sult [kən·sult′] *v.* When you consult someone, you ask him or her for information. **Daniel wanted to** *consult* **his coach about how he could jump higher.**

creep [krēp] *v.* **crept** If you crept, you moved slowly and carefully so that you wouldn't be seen or heard. **The cat** *crept* **up behind the mouse.** *syn.* sneak

creep

a	add	e	end	o	odd	o͞o	pool	oi	oil	th	this		a in *above*
ā	ace	ē	equal	ō	open	u	up	ou	pout	zh	vision	ə =	e in *sicken*
â	care	i	it	ô	order	û	burn	ng	ring				i in *possible*
ä	palm	ī	ice	o͝o	took	yo͞o	fuse	th	thin				o in *melon*
													u in *circus*

criticize [krit′ə·sīz′] *v.* When you criticize something, you tell what you think is wrong with it. **Sergio was glad that the art teacher did not *criticize* his painting.**

cul·ture [kul′chər] *n.* A culture is made up of a group's customs and traditions. **In North American *culture*, people shake hands when they meet.**

cun·ning [kun′ing] *adj.* Someone who is cunning uses smart and tricky ways to get what he or she wants. **The *cunning* fox crept into the chicken house after dark.** *syns.* sly, crafty

cu·ri·os·i·ty [kyŏŏr′ē·os′ə·tē] *n.* Something that is called a curiosity is something odd or unusual that interests people. **The flower's blooming in winter was a *curiosity*.** *syn.* oddity

dazed [dāzd] *adj.* If you are dazed, you are confused and cannot think properly. **The winner was *dazed* by the surprise announcement and didn't know what to say.**

de·cent [dē′sənt] *adj.* Someone who is decent is good and fair. **Cameron is a *decent* person who always treats his customers honestly.** *syns.* kind, respectable

de·lib·er·a·tion [di·lib′ə·rā′shən] *n.* Deliberation is thought and discussion that comes before making a decision. **After much *deliberation*, the judges gave the award to Jordan.** *syns.* consideration, thought

de·light·ed [di·līt′id] *adj.* When you are very happy about something, you are delighted. **Sofia was *delighted* when she got an A on her test.**

delighted

syns. overjoyed, thrilled

dem·on·strate [dem′ən·strāt′] *v.* When you demonstrate something, you show how it works or how it is done. **Adrianne will *demonstrate* a basketball trick.** *syn.* show

demonstrate

de·tail [dē′tāl] *n.* A detail is a small piece of information that is part of a larger whole. **Jada planned every *detail* of her party.**

de·vise [di·vīz′] *v.* To devise is to figure out a way to do something. **Emma needed to *devise* a way to get her chores finished.** *syn.* invent

di·a·logue [dī′ə·lôg′] *n.* Conversation between people is called dialogue. **The two actors had a lot of *dialogue* to memorize for the play.**

--- Word Origins ---

dialogue *Dialogue* means "conversation." To begin with, it came from the Greek word *diálogos*. The prefix *dia-* means "across or between," and the root *légein* means "speak." So, to speak between people is to have a conversation or dialogue.

dim [dim] *adj.* It is dim when there is not much light. **The *dim* light of the room made it difficult for Leslie to read.**

din [din] *n.* If there is a din, there is so much noise that it is hard to hear anything over it. **The *din* of the crowd made it hard to hear my friend talk.** *syn.* racket

dis·ap·point·ed [dis′ə·point′ed] *adj.* You are disappointed if you are unhappy about the way something turned out. **Elijah was *disappointed* that his team lost the game.** *syns.* saddened, upset

dis·grace·ful [dis·grās′fəl] *adj.* If something is disgraceful, it is shocking and not acceptable. **James thought his poor performance in the game was *disgraceful*.** *syns.* dreadful, shameful

dis·guise [dis·gīz′] *v.* **dis·guised** If you are disguised, you are wearing something that keeps people from knowing who you are. **Maya was *disguised* by a mask when she came to the costume party.** *syn.* camouflage

disguise

dis·miss [dis·mis′] *v.* To dismiss is to give permission to leave. **Savannah hopes the teacher will *dismiss* the class early for recess.**

dis·solve [di·zolv′] *v.* When something dissolves, it mixes completely with a liquid. **The powder will *dissolve* if you stir it into water.**

dodge [doj] *v.* **dodg·ing** When you are dodging something, you avoid something that is coming toward you. **Fast runners are usually good at *dodging* the ball.** *syn.* avoid

do·nate [dō′nāt′] *v.* **do·nat·ed** Something that has been donated has been given away for free. **Many parents *donated* flowers to be planted in front of the school.**

doze [dōz] *v.* **doz·es** Someone who dozes takes short naps. **The baby usually *dozes* in her crib after she eats.** *syns.* sleep, snooze

drift [drift] *v.* **drifts** When something drifts, it moves along without direction. **Mikayla watches as the boat *drifts* down the stream.** *syn.* float

drow·sy [drou′zē] *adj.* When you are drowsy, you feel so sleepy that you can't stay awake. **Although Andrew got plenty of sleep, he still felt *drowsy*.** *syns.* sleepy, tired

---

E

ef·fort [ef′ərt] *n.* When you work hard, you use effort. **It took a lot of *effort* to clean up the playground after the storm.** *syn.* work

el·e·va·ted [el′ə·vā′ted] *adj.* Something that is elevated is lifted up. **The *elevated* walkway lets people cross the street by walking above it.** *syn.* raised

ACADEMIC LANGUAGE

> **e-mail** An *e-mail* is a written message sent from one computer to another.

em·bar·rass [im·bar′əs] *v.* If you embarrass someone, you make that person feel uncomfortable or ashamed. **Courtney will *embarrass* herself if she forgets her lines in the play.**

em·brace [im·brās′] *v.* **em·braced** If you hugged someone, you embraced that person. **Angela *embraced* her grandmother**  **as soon as she walked through the door.** *syns.* hug, squeeze

embrace

e·mo·tion [i·mō′shən] *n*. An emotion is a feeling, such as happiness. **Michael was filled with** *emotion* **when he found out that the book had belonged to his great-grandfather.** *syn*. feeling

en·cour·ag·ing [in·kûr′ij·ing] *adj*. Something that is encouraging gives someone hope or confidence. **The coach's speech before the championship game was** *encouraging*. *syn*. hopeful

e·nor·mous [i′nôr′məs] *adj*. Something that is enormous is very big. **The elephant's footprints were** *enormous*. *syns*. huge, gigantic

e·rupt [i·rupt′] *v*. Something that erupts breaks out of something that holds it. **Lava will** *erupt* **when the pressure inside the volcano becomes too great.**

— **Word Origins** —

erupt This word is borrowed from the Latin word *ēruptus* or *ērumpere,* which means "to break out or burst forth."

ev·i·dence [ev′ə·dəns] *n*. Evidence is proof that something has happened. **The footprints were** *evidence* **that deer had been in the yard.** *syns*. proof, confirmation

ex·claim [iks·klām′] *v*. **ex·claimed** If you exclaimed something, you said it excitedly. **"I can't believe we won!"** Elizabeth *exclaimed*.

ex·pand [ik·spand′] *v*. When things expand, they get bigger. **We watched the balloon** *expand* **as the air filled it.** *syn*. swell

ex·pert [ek′spûrt] *n*. An expert is someone who knows a lot about a certain subject. **The quarterback is an** *expert* **at throwing a football.**

ACADEMIC LANGUAGE

expository nonfiction *Expository nonfiction* explains information and ideas.

expression Reading aloud with *expression* means using your voice to match the action of the story and the character's feelings.

a add	e end	o odd	o͞o pool	oi oil	th this	
ā ace	ē equal	ō open	u up	ou pout	zh vision	ə = a in *above*, e in *sicken*, i in *possible*, o in *melon*, u in *circus*
â care	i it	ô order	û burn	ng ring		
ä palm	ī ice	o͝o took	yo͞o fuse	th thin		

ACADEMIC LANGUAGE

fable A *fable* is a short story that teaches a lesson about life, often using animals that act like people.

fairy tale A *fairy tale* is a story that takes place in a make-believe world.

fa·mine [fam′in] *n.* When there is famine, there is not enough food to feed everyone. **Hot, dry weather for a long period of time can cause *famine* in an area.**

ACADEMIC LANGUAGE

fantasy A *fantasy* is a story that could not happen in real life.

flick [flik] *v.* When you flick something, you move it or snap it quickly. **The frog can *flick* its tongue to catch a bug.** *syn.* snap

flick

flus·ter [flus′tər] *v.* flus·tered If something flustered you, it made you forget what you were saying or doing. **It flustered Oscar to have so many people watching him.** *syns.* distract, confuse

flut·ter [flut′ər] *v.* **flut·ter·ing** When something moves through the air lightly and quickly, it is fluttering. **The moth's wings were *fluttering* as it flew around the light.** *syn.* flap

ACADEMIC LANGUAGE

folktale A *folktale* is a story that has been passed down through time.

fondness [fond′nəs] *n.* If you like something very much, you have a fondness for it. **Hayley has a *fondness* for fresh pineapple.** *syns.* weakness, affection

func·tion·al [fungk′shən·əl] *adj.* Something that serves a purpose is functional. **The birthday gift, a sweater, was both pretty and *functional*.** *syn.* practical

gaze [gāz] *n.* A gaze is a long look at something. **Gabriella's *gaze* was directed at the sky.** *syn.* stare

gen·er·ate [jen′ə·rāt′] *v.* **gen·er·ates** To generate something is to produce it. **We bought a machine that *generates* electricity.** *syn.* produce

gen·er·ous [jen′ər·əs] *adj.* People who are generous are happy to share with others. **Justin was *generous* when he shared his lunch after Desiree forgot hers.** *syn.* giving

glance [glans] *v.* **glanc·ing** When you are glancing at something, you are taking a quick look at it. **Tyler kept *glancing* at the clock to see how much time was left.** *syns.* look, glimpse

glimpse [glimps] *n.* When you get a glimpse of something, you get only a quick peek at it. **Anthony got a *glimpse* of his birthday cake in the box.** *syn.* peek

── Word Origins ──

glimpse *Glimpse* comes from the German word *glim* which meant "to shine softly" or "to see a soft flash."

glo·ri·ous [glôr′ē·əs] *adj.* If something is so wonderful that you can hardly believe it, it is glorious. **The cake was a *glorious* surprise for Jackson's birthday.** *syns.* wonderful, splendid

grain·y [grā′nē] *adj.* If something is grainy, it is not smooth but has many small, hard pieces. **When Donald mixed the paint with sand, it felt *grainy*.** *syn.* gritty

groom [groom] **1.** *v.* **grooms** When an animal grooms itself, it makes itself neat and clean. **Angelica's cat *grooms* itself by licking its fur.** *syn.* clean **2.** *n.* A groom is a man who is being married or was just married. **The *groom* stood quietly as the wedding music began.**

heave [hēv] *v.* **heav·ing** Heaving means throwing something heavy with great effort. **Davion needs help *heaving* this heavy bag onto the truck.** *syn.* throw

a add	e end	o odd	o͞o pool	oi oil	t͟h this	a in *above*
ā ace	ē equal	ō open	u up	ou pout	zh vision	e in *sicken*
â care	i it	ô order	û burn	ng ring		ə = i in *possible*
ä palm	ī ice	o͝o took	yo͞o fuse	th thin		o in *melon*
						u in *circus*

he·ro·ic [hi·rō´ik] *adj.* Someone who is heroic is brave and acts like a hero. **The mayor thanked the firefighter for her *heroic* act.** *syns.* courageous, brave

hin·der [hin´dər] *v.* When you hinder someone, you make it difficult or impossible for them to do something. **Tiana's sore ankle won't *hinder* her from finishing the race.** *syn.* stop

ACADEMIC LANGUAGE

historical fiction *Historical fiction* is a made-up story that is set in the past with people, places, and events that did happen or could have happened.

how- to article A *how-to article* gives step-by-step instructions for completing a task or project.

im·merse [i·mûrs´] *v.* To immerse oneself is to become very involved in something. **Alexis would *immerse* herself in any book she was reading.** *syn.* sink

in·de·pen·dent [in´di·pen´dənt] *adj.* A person who is independent is someone who does things on his or her own. **Learning to tie his shoes made my little brother more *independent*.**

ACADEMIC LANGUAGE

informational narrative *Informational narrative* presents information in the form of a story.

in·hab·i·tant [in·hab´ə·tənt] *n.* **in·hab·i·tants** The people or animals that live in a certain place are the inhabitants of that place. **Two little goldfish were the only *inhabitants* of the fishbowl.** *syn.* occupant

in·her·it [in·her´it] *v.* When you inherit something, you have been given something by someone who used to own it. **Brittany will *inherit* her sister's bicycle when her sister grows too tall for it.**

ACADEMIC LANGUAGE

interview An *interview* is a conversation in which one person asks questions and another person gives answers.

intonation *Intonation* is the rise and fall of your voice as you read aloud.

in·ven·tion [in·ven´shən] *n.* An invention is something completely new that someone has made. **The scientist's *invention* will make life easier for everyone.**

in·ves·ti·gate [in·ves′tə·gāt′] *v.* When you investigate something, you try to find out the truth about it. **Tyler had to *investigate* the disappearance of his lunch box.**

is·sue [ish′oo] *n.* An issue is an edition of a newspaper or magazine. **Carlos was excited when the latest *issue* of his favorite magazine came in the mail.**

ACADEMIC LANGUAGE

journal A *journal* is a personal record of daily events.

lab·o·ra·to·ry [lab′rə·tôr′ē] *n.* A place where experiments are done is a laboratory. **The scientist bought some brand-new equipment for his *laboratory*.**

ACADEMIC LANGUAGE

legend A *legend* is a story from the past that is often partly true.

loy·al [loi′əl] *adj.* Someone who is loyal stands by you in good times and bad. **Caleb's dog is *loyal* to him.** *syn.* faithful

ACADEMIC LANGUAGE

magazine article A *magazine article* is a short selection that appears in a magazine and gives information about a topic.

mag·ni·fy [mag′nə·fī′] *v.* When you magnify something, you make it look larger than it actually is. **Noah used the microscope to *magnify* the surface of the leaf.** *syn.* enlarge

man·da·to·ry [man′də·tôr′ē] *adj.* Something that is mandatory is required. **Mr. Greene said that writing the book report is *mandatory*.** *syns.* necessary, required

a	add	e	end	o	odd	o͞o	pool	oi	oil	th	this		a in *above*
ā	ace	ē	equal	ō	open	u	up	ou	pout	zh	vision		e in *sicken*
â	care	i	it	ô	order	û	burn	ng	ring			ə =	i in *possible*
ä	palm	ī	ice	o͝o	took	yo͞o	fuse	th	thin				o in *melon*
													u in *circus*

maze [māz] *n.* A maze is a winding set of paths that is like a puzzle. **Finding my way around town was like being lost in a *maze.***

mem·o·ry [mem′ər·ē] *n.* A memory is something you remember. **Maria's favorite *memory* was the day her dad brought home a new puppy.** *syn.* remembrance

men·tion [men′shən] *v.* **men·tioned** If you mentioned something, you talked about it briefly. **David *mentioned* wanting to be the first to try the new computer game.** *syns.* say, remark

midst [midst] *n.* If you are in the midst of something, you are in the middle of it. **Andrew and Marissa were in the *midst* of discussing their project.**

mo·del [mod′əl] *v.* **mo·deled** If you modeled something, you showed it so that others could see it. **Francisco *modeled* his costume for the class.** *syn.* show, present

mur·mur [mûr′mûr] *v.* **mur·mured** When people murmur, they speak so softly that they can hardly be heard. **Trevor could not hear what Nia *murmured* to herself.** *syn.* mumble

ACADEMIC LANGUAGE

mystery In a *mystery*, something strange happens that is not explained until the end of the story.

myth A *myth* is a story that shows what a group of people in the past believed about how something came to be.

ACADEMIC LANGUAGE

news feature A *news feature* gives information—about a person or topic—in a newspaper or magazine.

newsletter A *newsletter* presents information—about an organization—to a person or group of people.

news script A *news script* is a text that is read aloud and gives information about important events.

noc·tur·nal [nok·tûr′nəl] *adj.* An animal that is nocturnal sleeps during the day and is active at night. **Raccoons and opossums are active at night because they are *nocturnal* animals.**

Word Origins

nocturnal The Latin word *nox* means "night," and *nocturnes* means "belonging to the night."

ACADEMIC LANGUAGE

nonfiction *Nonfiction* gives facts and information about people, places, or things.

nui·sance [noo͞′səns] *n.* Something or someone that bothers you can be a nuisance. **The neighbor's barking dog was a *nuisance*.** *syns.* pest, irritation

o·bey [ō·bā′] *v.* When you obey, you do what you are told to do. **Good citizens *obey* the law.**

o·blige [ə·blīj′] *v.* When you oblige someone, you help the person. **Austin is always happy to *oblige* when anyone needs help spelling a word.** *syns.* help, assist

ob·serve [əb·zûrv′] *v.* **ob·served** If you observed something, you watched it carefully to learn more about it. **Elijah *observed* the tree's**

changes in each season. *syns.* study, examine

ACADEMIC LANGUAGE

online information *Online information* is found on an Internet website.

o·ver·hear [ō′vər·hir′] *v.* **o·ver·heard** If you overheard what people said, you heard it without their knowing that you were listening. **Amir *overheard* his sister talking on the phone.**

ACADEMIC LANGUAGE

pace Reading at an appropriate *pace* means reading at the right speed.

par·ti·cle [pär′ti·kəl] *n.* **par·ti·cles** Tiny pieces of something are called particles. **Cody wiped the dust *particles* off the computer screen** *syn.* bit

a	add	e	end	o	odd	o͞o	pool	oi	oil	ŧħ	this
ā	ace	ē	equal	ō	open	u	up	ou	pout	zh	vision
â	care	i	it	ô	order	û	burn	ng	ring		
ä	palm	ī	ice	o͝o	took	yo͞o	fuse	th	thin		

ə = { a in *above* / e in *sicken* / i in *possible* / o in *melon* / u in *circus*

patch·work [pach′wûrk′] *n.*
Patchwork is cloth made by sewing together small pieces of different fabrics. **The quilt Grandma made is a *patchwork* of pieces cut from the family's old clothing.**

patchwork

pa·trol [pə·trōl′] *v.* People patrol an area to watch over and guard it. **Police *patrol* a neighborhood to keep it safe.** *syns.* tour, watch, guard

per·ma·nent [pûr′mən·ənt] *adj.*
per·ma·nent·ly If something stays one way forever, it stays that way permanently. **The statue was set in the ground *permanently* so that it could not be moved.**

ACADEMIC LANGUAGE

photo essay A *photo essay* presents information mostly with photographs and with some text.

phrasing *Phrasing* is the grouping of words into small "chunks," or phrases, when you read aloud.

pic·tur·esque [pik′chə·resk′] *adj.*
Something that is picturesque is pretty enough to be in a picture. **The old village with its colorful flowers and little cottages was *picturesque*.** *syn.* charming

ACADEMIC LANGUAGE

play A *play* is a story written so that it can be performed for an audience.

pleas·ant [plez′ənt] *adj.* Something that is pleasant is enjoyable and makes you happy. **The weather is *pleasant* today.**

plen·ty [plen′tē] *n.* If you have plenty of something, you have more than enough. **There are *plenty* of toys for everyone.**

ACADEMIC LANGUAGE

poetry *Poetry* uses rhythm and imagination to express feelings and ideas.

postcards *Postcards* can be mailed without an envelope and usually have a picture on one side.

praise [prāz] *v.* **praised** If you have praised someone, you have told that person that he or she did something well. **The teacher *praised* the students for their fine drawings.**

prey [prā] *n.* An animal that is hunted for food is prey. **The zebra became *prey* for a hungry lion.**

pro·tect [prə·tekt′] *v.* **pro·tects** When you protect something, you keep it safe. **Amir *protects* his head by wearing a bicycle helmet.** *syns.* guard, defend

--- **Word Origins** ---

protect *Protect* comes from the Latin word *prōtegere.* The prefix *pro-* means "in front" and the root word *tegere* means "cover." So when you protect someone, you cover him or her from the front like a shield.

ACADEMIC LANGUAGE

punctuation Paying attention to *punctuation,* such as commas and periods, will help you read a text correctly.

ACADEMIC LANGUAGE

reading rate Your *reading rate* is how quickly you can read a text correctly and still understand what you are reading.

realistic fiction *Realistic fiction* is a story that could happen in real life.

re·cite [ri·sīt′] *v.* **re·ci·ted** If you recited something, you memorized it and then spoke it aloud. **Ali *recited* the names of all 50 states without looking at a map.**

rec·om·mend [rek′ə·mend′] *v.* When you recommend something, you tell someone that you think it is good. **Alexis asked her teacher to *recommend* a book to read.**

reel [rēl] *v.* **reels 1.** A person reels something in by winding up a line attached to it. **Brian watches as Grandma *reels* in a big fish.** *syn.* pull **2.** When a person reels, he or she feels dizzy and sways from side to side. **Kevin *reels* after stepping off a carousel.** *syns.* sway, stagger

a	add	e	end	o	odd	o͞o	pool	oi	oil	th	this		a in *above*
ā	ace	ē	equal	ō	open	u	up	ou	pout	zh	vision		e in *sicken*
â	care	i	it	ô	order	û	burn	ng	ring			ə =	i in *possible*
ä	palm	ī	ice	o͝o	took	yo͞o	fuse	th	thin				o in *melon*
													u in *circus*

re·flect [ri·flekt′] *v.* **re·flects 1.** When something reflects light, the light bounces off the surface instead of passing through it. **A mirror *reflects* an image of whatever is in front of it. 2.** When someone reflects, he or she thinks about something that happened in the past. **Ryan *reflects* on what he has learned and then writes about it in his journal.**

reflect

re·hearse [ri·hûrs′] *v.* To rehearse is to practice for a performance. **Jasmine wanted to *rehearse* her lines for the play.** *syn.* practice

re·mark [ri·märk′] *n.* A remark is something that is said about something. **Karen was pleased with the kind *remark* Ms. Hill had written on her paper.** *syns.* comment, statement

re·pair [ri·pâr′] *n.* **re·pairs** When something needs repairs, it needs to be fixed. **Cynthia needs to make *repairs* to her bike before the race.**

re·quire [ri·kwīr′] *v.* **re·quired** Something that is required is needed. **Each member of the baseball team is *required* to attend all the practices.**

re·search [ri·sûrch′ or rē′sûrch′] *n.* Research involves getting information about a question or topic. **Isabel has done *research* on desert animals for her report.** *syn.* study

re·source [ri·sôrs′ or rē′sôrs′] *n.* **re·sour·ces** Resources are materials, money, and other things that can be used. **Water *resources* are important to cities.** *syn.* supply

re·spon·si·bil·i·ty [ri·spon′sə·bil′ə·tē] *n.* A responsibility is something you are expected to do. **It was Trevor's *responsibility* to collect the tennis rackets after the game.** *syns.* duty, job

ri·dic·u·lous [ri·dik′yə·ləs] *adj.* Something that is very silly is ridiculous. **Brandon laughed at the *ridiculous* joke his mom told him.**

roost [rō̄ost] *v.* Birds roost, or perch, when they sleep in trees at night. **Many birds *roost* in the tree outside my window each night.**

ro·tate [rō′tāt] *v.* **ro·tates**
Something that rotates spins like
a top. **Earth *rotates* on its axis
once every 24 hours.**

ru·in [rōō′in] *v.* **ru·ined** If
something is ruined, it is no longer
any good. **Devin's shirt was
ruined when he accidentally
spilled paint on it.** *syn.* spoil

rus·tle [rus′əl] *v.* **rust·ling** When
objects are rustling, they are
moving and making soft sounds.
**Please stop *rustling* those
papers.**

S

safe·guard [sāf′gärd′] *v.* To
safeguard something is to protect
and guard it. **Emily brought
the potted plant indoors to
safeguard it from the cold.** *syn.*
protect

scarce [skârs] *adj.* Something is
scarce if there is not much of it to
be found. **Open land is *scarce* in
the crowded city.** *syn.* rare

scent [sent] *n.* A scent
is the smell of
something.
**Carol loves the
scent of spring
flowers.**
syns. odor, smell

scent

ACADEMIC LANGUAGE

science fiction *Science fiction*
is a made-up story using ideas
from science.

scold [skōld] *v.* **scold·ing** If you are
scolding someone, you are angrily
pointing out that person's mistakes.
**The mother is *scolding* her child
for misbehaving.**

sed·en·tar·y [sed′ən·târ′ē] *adj.*
If you have a sedentary job or
lifestyle, you are sitting down most
of the time. **The hen has become
sedentary since she laid her
eggs.** *syn.* inactive

sen·si·ble [sen′sə·bəl] *adj.* Someone
who is sensible makes good
decisions and judgments. **Jennifer
is a *sensible* eater who chooses
fruits as treats.** *syn.* wise

a	add	e	end	o	odd	ōō	pool	oi	oil	th	this		a in *above*
ā	ace	ē	equal	ō	open	u	up	ou	pout	zh	vision		e in *sicken*
â	care	i	it	ô	order	û	burn	ng	ring			ə =	i in *possible*
ä	palm	ī	ice	ōō	took	yōō	fuse	th	thin				o in *melon*
													u in *circus*

shab·by [shab′ē] *adj.* Shabby things look old and worn out. **This shabby coat will be fine for working in the garden.**

shal·low [shal′ō] *adj.* Something shallow is not very deep. **Stay in the shallow end of the pool.**

shel·ter [shel′tər] *v.* **shel·ters** Something that shelters you protects you and keeps you safe. **The tree's shade shelters us from the sun.** *syns.* protect, cover

sig·nal [sig′nəl] *n.* A signal is a sound or an action that sends a message. **The green light is a signal to go.** *syn.* sign

sob [sob] *v.* **sobbed** Someone who sobbed cried very hard. **Brenda sobbed when she lost her favorite book.** *syn.* cry

so·cial [sō′shəl] *adj.* A social animal is one that lives in a group with other animals of the same kind. **Monkeys are social animals that share the care of their young.**

sooth·ing [sooth′ing] *adj.* Something that is soothing makes you feel calm. **Jazmine thinks the sound of rain is soothing.** *syn.* calming

spear [spir] *v.* **spears** If someone spears something, he or she sticks something sharp through it. **Steven spears the green beans with his fork.** *syn.* stab

spi·ral [spī′rəl] *adj.* A spiral shape curls around and around in a circle. **The tornado looked like a spiral cloud.** *syns.* twisted, coiled

─── **Word Origins** ───

spiral The Latin *spiralis* means "to wind, coil, or twist." Today, the English *spiral* still has the same meaning.

sprin·kle [spring′kəl] *v.* **sprin·kled** Something that has been sprinkled has had tiny pieces or drops of something scattered all over it. **The blue floor that we had sprinkled with yellow paint was very colorful.**

squirm [skwûrm] *v.* **squirmed** If you squirmed in your seat, you kept wriggling around as if you were uncomfortable. **The puppy squirmed when Savion tried to pick it up.** *syn.* wriggle

stead·y [sted′ē] *adj.* A light that is steady always looks the same and does not change or go out. **The steady beam of the flashlight clearly showed the raccoon.** *syn.* continuous

strand [strand] *n.* **strands** Long, thin pieces of something are strands. **It is difficult to see the strands of a spiderweb.** *syn.* string

streak [strēk] *v.* To streak is to move very quickly from one place to another. **A falling star will *streak* across the sky.** *syns.* zoom, flash

strike [strīk] **1.** *v.* **strikes** If something strikes something else, it hits it. **Rod *strikes* a nail with his hammer.** *syn.* hit **2.** *n.* In baseball, a strike is a pitch that the batter misses. **After the third *strike,* Edward had to walk off the baseball field.**

strike

sug·gest [səg·jest´] *v.* **sug·gest·ed** If you suggested something, you gave someone an idea. **Ethan *suggested* that we finish our homework before dinner.** *syn.* recommend

sum·mon [sum´ən] *v.* **sum·mon·ing** If you are summoning someone, you are calling for the person to come. **Vanessa was *summoning* her brother to the table.** *syns.* beckon, call

sup·pose [sə·pōz´] *v.* When you suppose something, you think it is true. **What do you *suppose* will happen tomorrow?** *syn.* believe

sur·face [sûr´fis] *n.* The surface of something is the top part of it. **Dolphins must come up to the *surface* of the water to breathe.**

Word Origins

surface What does your face have to do with the word *surface? Surface* was originally a French word. The prefix *sur-* means "above," and *face* means "face." So, since a face is what we see as the front and top of something, a surface is the top or outer part of something.

---

sur·vive [sər·vīv´] *v.* To survive is to remain alive, even after great difficulties. **Living things need food, water, air, and shelter to *survive*.** *syn.* live

sus·pect [sə·spekt´] *v.* When you suspect someone of doing something, you think that person has done it. **Knowing her brother made Emily *suspect* that he had eaten all the cookies.**

a	add	e	end	o	odd	o͞o	pool	oi	oil	t͟h	this		a in *above*
ā	ace	ē	equal	ō	open	u	up	ou	pout	zh	vision		e in *sicken*
â	care	i	it	ô	order	û	burn	ng	ring			ə =	i in *possible*
ä	palm	ī	ice	o͝o	took	yo͞o	fuse	th	thin				o in *melon*
													u in *circus*

143

sway [swā] *v.* When things sway, they swing slowly back and forth. **The branches *sway* back and forth in the breeze.** *syn.* swing

swift [swift] *adj.* Something that is swift moves very quickly. **The *swift* runner finished the race quickly.** *syns.* fast, rapid

swoop [swo͞op] *v.* **swoops** When something swoops, it dives or dips downward. **The pelican *swoops* toward the water to catch a fish.** *syns.* dive, plunge

swoop

ACADEMIC LANGUAGE

syllable A *syllable* is the smallest part of a word that contains a single vowel sound.

tal·ent·ed [tal′ən·tid] *adj.* A talented person has the special ability to do something very well. **Serena is a very *talented* drummer.** *syns.* skilled, gifted

ten·der [ten′dər] *adj.* Something, like food, that is tender is soft and easy to chew or cut. **The meat was *tender* and juicy.**

ACADEMIC LANGUAGE

textbook A *textbook* is a book that is used in schools to teach a subject.

thor·ough [thûr′ō] *adj.* If you do something in a thorough way, you do a careful and complete job. **James gave his room a *thorough* cleaning.** *syns.* complete, careful

ACADEMIC LANGUAGE

time line A *time line* is a line that shows dates of past events in the order in which they happened.

trans·late [trans·lāt′] *v.* If you translate something, you say or write it in another language. **Can Kimberly *translate* this letter into English?** *syn.* interpret

ACADEMIC LANGUAGE

travel journal A *travel journal* is a personal record of events that happen while going from one place to another.

tu·tor [tōō′tər] *n.* A tutor is someone who helps another person with schoolwork. **César has a math *tutor* to help him after school.** *syns.* teacher, instructor

U

u·ni·form [yōō′nə·fôrm′] *n.* **u·ni·forms** Uniforms are clothes that all the people in a group wear so that they are dressed alike. **Ian could tell his teammates by their *uniforms*.**

uniform

Word Origins

uniform This word comes from the Latin word *uniformis* meaning "one form." If everyone wears only one form of clothing, they are wearing a uniform.

V

vain [vān] *adj.* If you are vain, you think very highly of yourself. **The *vain* boy spent a lot of time thinking about how handsome he was.** *syns.* conceited, arrogant

var·i·ous [vâr′ē·əs] *adj.* When there are various objects, there are objects of different types. **The box was full of *various* items that students had lost.** *syn.* assorted

ver·sion [vûr′zhən] *n.* **ver·sions** If there are different versions of a story, the story is told in different ways. **Sean wondered if the second *version* of his short story was better than the first.**

Word Origins

version The word *version* comes from the Latin *versionem,* which means "a turning." So when you hear a new version of a story, it has made a turn and is told in another way.

---

a	add	e	end	o	odd	ōō	pool	oi	oil	th	this		*a* in *above*
ā	ace	ē	equal	ō	open	u	up	ou	pout	zh	vision	ə =	*e* in *sicken*
â	care	i	it	ô	order	û	burn	ng	ring				*i* in *possible*
ä	palm	ī	ice	ōō	took	yōō	fuse	th	thin				*o* in *melon*
													u in *circus*

view·er [vyoo′ər] *n.* **view·ers** Viewers are people who watch something. **The host of the show told stories that were interesting to his *viewers*.**

vis·i·ble [viz′ə·bəl] a*dj.* When something is visible, you can see it. **The fireworks were *visible* for miles around.** *syn.* noticeable

visible

wan·der [wän′dər] *v.* **wan·ders** A person who wanders travels without planning where he or she is going. **The tourist *wanders,* stopping at places of interest around town.**

whine [hwīn] *v.* **whined** If someone or something whined, it gave a long, high cry. **The toddler *whined* when his mother would not buy the toy.** *syn.* whimper

yank [yangk] *v.* yanked If you yanked something, you gave it a quick, hard pull. **The man *yanked* on the cord to start the boat's motor.** *syns.* tug, pull

Photo Credits

Illustration Credits